AF263691

Ancient India

Discovering Lost Stories from Indian History

Free Bonus from Captivating History (Available for a Limited time)

Hi History Lovers!

Now you have a chance to join our exclusive history list so you can get your first history ebook for free as well as discounts and a potential to get more history books for free!

Simply visit the link below to join.

Or, Scan the QR code!

captivatinghistory.com/ebook

Also, make sure to follow us on Facebook, X, and YouTube by searching for Captivating History.

Table of Contents

Introduction

The Indian subcontinent was already alive around the same time the great pyramids were beginning to rise along the Nile. By the third millennium BCE, cities began to dot along the Indus and its tributaries, transforming the region completely. Some would consider these cities ahead of their time, as they were constructed with meticulous details.

More often than not, their streets were laid out on a grid, straight and evenly measured. Houses typically featured private wells and bathing areas. Most of the cities even had their own drainage system that ran beneath the streets, concealed with bricks and cleaned through inspection points. This was something the world would not see again in most places for thousands of years! It's safe to say that the Indus was one of the world's earliest urban civilizations, yet sadly, many people today know far less about it than they do about Egypt or Mesopotamia.

The reason behind this is rather simple. Unlike the history of the Greeks or the Egyptians, much of early Indian history was not written down in a steady line of records. Instead, the people of the Indus Valley preserved their past in different ways. Although foreign visitors kept records of what they saw across the subcontinent, these came from their own viewpoints. Greek writers described the lands they reached in the time of Alexander, while Chinese pilgrims wrote about their travels to Buddhist centers. The subcontinent was also mentioned in Persian records, though they were merely described as territories the Persians sought to influence. True, these accounts are useful, but they show India through outside eyes.

Within India itself, memory often lived in stories. This is where major epics like the *Rāmāyaṇa* and the *Mahābhārata* come in. These accounts are more than just long poems and mystical tales. In fact, they belong to a tradition called *Itihasa*—directly translated as "thus indeed it was." Importantly, *Itihasa* does not separate history from meaning in the same way modern books do. Instead, it carries memories of the past woven together with questions of duty, belief, and the nature of the world.

Of course, this does not mean that India lacked real events or real kingdoms. It simply means that storytelling was one of the ways people understood their past. Some characters may be based on historical figures. Some battles may mirror real conflicts. Over time, these memories blended with spiritual lessons and symbolic ideas. The result is a landscape where the line between what happened and what was believed is not rigid but fluid, understood differently depending on the tradition.

But it is this blending of history and story that makes ancient India so fascinating. Rather than relying only on dusty records or monuments, it invites us to explore a world where poetry, ritual, memory, and power all shaped the way people saw themselves. In the following pages, we'll explore what archaeology has uncovered, what foreign visitors have observed, what Indian traditions have preserved in their own voices, and of course, the interpretations of modern scholars.

Some tales are well known. Others are rarely retold, overshadowed by mainstream history. Together, they reveal a civilization that has continued to evolve for thousands of years, carrying its stories forward even when its cities fell silent.

Chapter 1 – Porus and Alexander the Great

The old ones called the river flowing through India and Pakistan the Parushni. To us, it's the Ravi River. And about three thousand years ago, along its banks, stood two great coalitions of men. On one side stood King Sudas of the Bharatas. He was young, but he commanded a clan that guarded the heart of the Punjab. Meanwhile, on the other side were ten kings who had joined arms, bound more by jealousy than by friendship. These kings were eager to see one thing: a blade buried deep into the heart of King Sudas and his men.

The Ravi River today.[1]

The ten came from every horizon. While Purus and Druhyus rode all the way from the west, Yadus and Turvaśas came from the south and Anus from the north. These, however, were the only names that survived the test of time, mentioned in the *Rigveda* (the oldest of the sacred books of Hinduism).

This rivalry with King Sudas and the Bharatas was not always there. Interestingly, the Bharatas (an early Vedic tribe prominent especially in the latter half of the second millennium BCE) had once been part of the alliance. But when Sudas's power grew tremendously, eventually threatening the old balance of power in the region, resentment began to brew. Then came priestly rivalry, which eventually sparked the conflict. It boiled to the maximum temperature when the Bharatas' king replaced his former chief priest, Vishwamitra, with his own favored priest, Vasishtha.

Swearing revenge, Vishwamitra orchestrated the battle. He began whispering into the ears of the leaders of neighboring clans, reminding them of the havoc that would engulf the region as long as Sudas sat on the throne. He urged them to unite against the Bharatas' king. And so, the ten gathered their forces and strength and crossed the river plains. They were confident that their numbers alone could easily drown Sudas's small but disciplined force. The story, however, had another ending for them.

One could only imagine the air before the battle broke out. The priests of Sudas turned to the divine, burning ghee upon the sacred fire and praying to Indra (the Hindu deity of weather) for divine intervention. The opposing kings chanted for the same god's favor, hoping Indra would be on their side as they obliterated their enemy.

When the battle opened at dawn, the sky shivered with thunder. Arrows hissed as the atmosphere was filled with the sounds of spears striking shields and chariots charging across the riverbanks. According to the *Rigveda*, divine intervention did occur. Rain soon came pouring down, swelling the Parushni and threatening the forces of the ten kings. It seemed as if the gods were siding with the Bharatas after all. The floods rose suddenly, cutting off their retreat. Chariots sank into the mud, horses neighed desperately for life, and men were swallowed whole by the torrent. Sudas's warriors pressed the attack, and when the waters receded, the ten kings lay broken.

The victory was absolute. Sudas emerged as the mightiest ruler of the Vedic world, and the Bharatas became the dominant tribe of the northern plains. The defeated tribes scattered to other lands. While some merged with distant peoples, others vanished altogether into the dust of history.

The hymns that spoke of the battle made it sound completely divine, as if gods had chosen a side. But historians would absolutely agree that its roots were purely human. It all revolved around power, pride, and the shifting sands of allegiance. It is safe to say that India, even in her earliest age, was never a land of stillness. Kingdoms rose and fell along the rivers; priests and kings competed for favor and survival. And in the memory of the people, this particular event is remembered as India's first great war ever recorded.

But of course, the Battle of the Ten Kings was not the only one that once shook India. Many centuries later, another wave of news began to drift across the desert winds, coming from far beyond the mountains. It spoke of a certain conqueror who had been mercilessly marching from the far west. He had crushed Persia, crowned himself pharaoh of the Egyptians lands, and burned cities in Bactria. Some called him "Master of the World," while those who knew him personally knew him by his name, Alexander of Macedon.

When Alexander's scouts first glimpsed the shining waters of the Hydaspes, they thought they were entering an unknown world. But the rivers of India had long witnessed wars before the Greeks were ever a people. The Parushni had swallowed ten kings. The Hydaspes would soon test another greater one.

The Threat from the West

When the people along the Indus learned more and more about the impending threat that loomed over them, they began to feel a surge of panic. Merchants closed their accounts early, and village headmen gathered at the temples, while the holy priests continued to read omens in the smoke. They were certain that the age of great invasions was returning, testing the courage of the people once more—though this time, the invader came not from a rival tribe or a neighboring kingdom, as during the Vedic wars. He came from the edge of the known world.

The chroniclers of Gandhara wrote that the first scouts appeared like ghosts at dawn. They were not Persians, though some wore Persian armor. Their shields were round, their spears long, and they marched in straight ranks that moved as one. No local chiefs had ever seen soldiers with such discipline and organization. The most feared of all was the Macedonian phalanx. This solid wall of men armed with long spears was known to advance against the enemy in a tight formation so closely packed that only a few could slip between their shields without being struck down. Then came the horsemen, typically placed behind the phalanx. The Macedonians also had engineers, scribes, and baggage trains that stretched for miles. The sight of this foreign force was as impressive as it was unnerving.

But the Indians were not easily deterred. It took more than numbers and a display of discipline to break warriors who had faced floods, rival clans, wandering raiders, and the wild strength of their own land since childhood.

However, not all were ready to repel any attacks laid by this mighty invader—especially those in the northwest region of the Indian subcontinent, who were growing weary each day. There, the rulers gathered their counselors to debate. Some envoys urged caution; others spoke of alliance. To resist such an army, they said, would bring ruin. To submit might bring reward.

The people of Taxila, for one, preferred to get on the invaders' good side rather than standing their ground. The city was one of the wealthiest in the region. It was a melting pot of scholars and traders, a place where Greek, Persian, and Indian merchants met in peace, exchanging goods and ideas. Its ruler, King Ambhi (known to the Greeks as Taxiles) was already aware of Alexander's many victories and had also heard rumors of the conqueror's generous treatment to those who willingly submitted. So, the decision was clear. Without wasting more time, Ambhi sent gifts of gold, fine linen, and other sorts of wealth to the foreigner. And when the Macedonian army finally reached his borders, he extended his arms, welcoming them as allies.

Meanwhile, east of the Hydaspes River was another man whose stance contrasted greatly with Ambhi's. Known as Porus, he was the lord of the tribe called Paurava. According to ancient sources, he was not only older than Ambhi but also prouder. He descended from a line of warriors who had ruled the land since the time when Sudas fought against his ten rivals on the banks of Parushni. His people were described to be tall and his elephants mighty. It was not surprising that his court was fierce in its independence. So, when his messengers returned with news of Ambhi's surrender, Porus chose to stand his ground. He was headstrong in ensuring that no foreign ruler would ever cross his river alive.

So, a battle was on the horizon. The Indian armies under Porus were as varied as the lands they defended. Unlike the rigid Macedonian phalanx, which moved like a single creature, the Indian forces were like a living mosaic. There were infantry archers, chariot riders from the plains, mercenaries from the hills, and cavalry trained to fight alongside towering elephants.

Ever since his major campaign against the Persian Empire, Alexander and his men had been campaigning almost continuously for roughly seven to eight years. He eventually crossed the Hindu Kush and entered the Indus region sometime in mid-326 BCE, right as the monsoon season was beginning. This was a time of violent storms, swollen rivers, and heavy rain that undoubtedly disrupted movement. Coupling this with the exhaustion that came from the long campaigns and the unfamiliar terrain in India, Alexander's men were growing unimaginably weary. Still, Alexander was not planning to turn back.

The Hydaspes, already swollen by the monsoon, flowed between the two forces. Porus stood on the eastern bank, where he could be seen walking among his war elephants. Around him, the camp moved quietly. Archers could be seen repairing and fixing their bowstrings by dim lamplight, while on the other corner, warriors sat cross-legged, drawing symbols of protection on the wet sand. Old priests muttered prayers while burning incense, its smoke curling upward and vanished into the mist a minute later.

The Macedonians were also busy with their work on the other side of the river. The men labored in silence under the dark sky, hauling logs and lashing them into rafts. Despite the heavy rain that came and went in bursts, flattening their campfires and wetting the canvas of their tents, the soldiers never complained. Some cleaned their weapons; others stared into the water, listening to the hiss of rain on the current.

By midnight, the rain eased. The clouds began to thin, and the moon appeared, pale and uncertain, over the horizon. Porus returned to his tent, but with the looming battle, he failed to sleep. For days, Alexander had made his life difficult. Alexander had been sending small detachments to feign crossing at different points along the Hydaspes. Each time, Porus's scouts sounded the alarm, and the cavalry thundered to the banks. Yet when the Macedonians withdrew again and again,

Porus began to believe that these were nothing more than tricks to wear him down. Then, one night, the deception became real.

Alexander led a large force upstream, far from the main camp. Their movement could barely be heard since the rain muffled the sound of hooves and oars. Under the cover of night and guided by willing locals, the men made their way toward a wooded island that divided the river. When thunder rolled across the heavens at first light, the Macedonians wasted no time. They slipped into the water, shields above their heads and their horses swimming beside them. By the time the first Indian sentries noticed the glint of bronze through the fog, it was already too late.

The very moment the alarm was sounded, Porus made haste. He mounted his elephant and rode to the front. The ancient Greek historian Plutarch, for one, described how Porus stood like a tower on his massive elephant, directing his army from its back. His army was said to have assembled with remarkable speed. They did not panic despite the surprise attack, but rather, they moved like a trained machine. The elephants took their places in the center, forming a living wall. Behind them, archers lined up in dense ranks, bows strung and ready. The chariots rolled onto the plain, their wheels slicing through the wet soil. Cavalry gathered at both flanks, spears tipped with iron that gleamed even through the mist.

Although they had been through dozens of wars and battles throughout the many campaigns, the Macedonians had never seen an army like this. In their eyes, the Indian formation was equally strange and magnificent. The elephants swayed in place, their tusks sheathed in bronze. When their mahouts (traditional elephant riders) called, the elephants raised their trunks in unison as a response. It was indeed a sight to behold. When the massive creatures trumpeted, the sound was so deep and thunderous that some of the Macedonian horses responded by rearing and snorting.

When it was time for the battle, Alexander shouted orders to his phalanx. The long rows of spears then advanced, as steady as a tide. However, the ground soon proved to be a traitor to the Macedonians. The monsoon rains had turned the field into mud. So, their advance was not their proudest. Some slipped their shields; others found it hard to even walk as their sandals sank into the soft, wet ground.

Porus then unleashed his war elephants. They came at a lumbering charge, tusks lowered, trampling through mud and men alike. They crushed through the Macedonian front ranks, scattering the phalanx that had long been feared by many armies before. Even soldiers who had once faced the famed Persian Immortals now found themselves screaming at the sight of the towering elephants that were busy tossing men aside like rag dolls. Then came the volleys of arrows from the Indian lines, which almost immediately darkened the sky. Chariots sped forward, striking at the enemy flanks while cavalry wheeled around in sweeping arcs.

Porus charging into battle on his war elephant.[2]

The Macedonians tried to regroup, but Porus's men were everywhere. Although some were beginning to lose faith and hope, Alexander refused to retreat. He did not lose his composure. Ever observant, he managed to study every motion of the battlefield and every movement of his enemy. Despite the chaos, he noticed how the elephants, despite being fearsome, created gaps between their ranks as they advanced. Seeing this as an opportunity to turn the tides, he sent forward his light infantry composed of Agrianians and archers from Crete. These men were known for their speed and precision. Their task was simple: aim for the mahouts, who were perching high on the elephants' necks.

Now that the beasts began to falter, Alexander pressed on, accompanied by his Companion Cavalry. These horsemen circled wide, drawing the Indian riders into pursuit. Then he turned suddenly and struck at their flank. This, however, was not the end of the battle; in fact, it stretched for hours.

Porus, atop his elephant, fought at the center of the battlefield, visible to all. Arrows had struck his armor, and a spear had already grazed his shoulder, yet he paid no mind, refusing to descend and submit. When his mahout had been killed, Porus steered the creature himself, guiding it with his knees while he hurled spears into the flesh of his enemies with a strength that inspired his men.

Still, the Macedonians pressed harder, and eventually, the Indian lines began to weaken. The chariots soon became useless in the mud as their wheels stuck fast. Many elephants were wounded, and when panicked, they tended to turn on their own ranks. Porus watched as his formation began to break. Yet he would not yield.

The climax of the episode came when a spear finally pierced Porus's thigh. Blood ran down his armor. The great elephant beneath him began to show signs of collapse, as it had suffered multiple wounds. However, Porus remained mounted, striking down those who came near. His guards eventually fell one by one. Those few who remained quickly formed a ring around their king, swearing to protect him at all costs. But unfortunately, the Macedonians proved to be a mighty adversary after all. When the fighting ended, the field was a sea of broken weapons and fallen beasts. The riverbank was littered with bodies, their blood only washed away into the soil when rain returned later. The Macedonians had likewise suffered a great loss during the battle, but they had prevailed once more.

A painting depicting Alexander approaching Porus.[8]

Alexander himself rode through the wreckage on his trusty yet wounded steed, Bucephalus. He only came to a halt when he saw Porus on his elephant. True, he was visibly wounded and bleeding down his thigh, but Porus seemed unbroken. Ancient writers described how Alexander approached his opponent slowly. Soldiers from both sides stepped aside, uncertain whether they were witnessing the end of a battle or the meeting of equals. Porus, proud even in defeat, looked down at the invader who had crossed half the world to fight him.

"How do you wish to be treated?" Alexander may have asked the Indian king, perhaps through an interpreter.

Porus's reply was calm and steady. "Like a king."

"So shall it be," the conqueror said. Some said he even smiled, not in mockery but in respect.

Holding to his word, Alexander ordered that Porus's wounds be treated. Interestingly, the conqueror restored the lands to him. Alexander had long understood that ruling newly conquered territory required loyal local kings, not foreign administrators who knew nothing of the land. What's more, Porus had displayed great courage and discipline. It was clear that his people highly respected him. These qualities made him far more valuable as an ally than a defeated enemy. By granting him his kingdom, Alexander hoped to not only ensure stability on his eastern frontier but also place the region under a leader whose strength and authority would serve his ambitions without requiring his own constant presence.

Alexander planned to expand his influence deeper into the subcontinent. But fate seemed to disagree with his plans. First came the death of his horse shortly after the battle. Alexander then founded a city on the riverbank of Hydaspes and named it after Bucephalus. Next came the famous mutiny.

Although the Macedonians had won once more, their spirits had dulled. Many had seen death closer than ever before. They whispered that if one Porus could fight like a hundred men, what would await them deeper in India where mightier kingdoms still stood?

The Macedonians had heard stories of what lay beyond the rivers. The Nanda Empire, a realm so vast and rich, was said to possess armies that numbered in the thousands, with many more elephants. The soldiers grew silent when they heard the rumor. They were certain that Hydaspes was the beginning of their end.

Still, Alexander called on his generals and expressed his wish of new conquests. He spoke about marching east until they reached the edge of the ocean. To him, the horizon was never enough. His men had been loyal to him for years, but they, too, had their limits. After all those years of hardship, they longed to see home.

So, at the banks of the Hyphasis River, they halted, refusing to advance any further. It was a rebellion driven purely by exhaustion. For the first time, the conqueror faced an enemy he could not defeat, and it was his own weary army. Perhaps disappointed, the mighty conqueror withdrew to his tent. There he remained for three days, refusing food and speech. Outside, his soldiers waited, their resolve unshaken. When he finally emerged, his voice was calm, but his eyes had lost their fire.

"We will return," he said simply. "But we will return by another road."

The march back was more somber than triumphant. The army split into columns, with some sailing down the Indus and others cutting through the merciless desert. Disease and thirst claimed more lives than battle ever had. Villages that once watched in awe now turned away as the foreigners passed. Alexander himself was wounded again during a siege, struck by an arrow that pierced his lung. Though he recovered, the invincible image that had carried him across continents began to fade. Perhaps his men were right all along: Hydaspes was the beginning of the end.

When he finally reached Babylon, years later, he was nothing but a shadow of the man who had confidently crossed the Hydaspes. The great empire he had built stretched from Greece to India. True, it was vast, but it was also difficult to hold. Still, he spoke again of campaigns, this time into Arabia or even the western sea, but his body was already failing. Fever took him soon after, at only thirty-two years old.

Porus led a longer life than the Macedonian king, although his name was not immortalized as much as Alexander's. For a time, he ruled peacefully under Macedonian oversight, keeping order in the lands between the Hydaspes and the Acesines. What happened afterward, however, is rather blurry. A few Greek writers claim that Porus was later killed by another governor named Eudemus during the struggles that followed Alexander's death.

Even to this day, Porus remains one of the most debated figures in the history of ancient India. His name is known almost entirely through Greek records, and even those do not agree on who he truly was. The name "Porus" is generally seen as a Greek form of Paurava, a ruler from the Paurava kingdom that may have descended from the ancient Puru tribe mentioned in the *Rigveda*. This would connect him to the same Purus who fought King Sudas in the Battle of Ten Kings, the earliest recorded war in India.

The Puru people were an important tribe during the Vedic period. They controlled parts of what is now Punjab, a region rich in water and fertile land. By the fourth century BCE, these old tribal divisions had developed into small kingdoms. The Paurava realm, if it was indeed ruled by Porus, likely stood between the rivers Hydaspes and Acesines in the area now called Jhelum in modern Pakistan. It was known for its elephants, horses, and strong agricultural base. Its location made it an important link between Central Asia and the Indian plains.

Historians do not agree on the size or importance of Porus's kingdom. Some believe he ruled a wide territory that included nearby regions such as Taxila, while others think his power was more limited but still strategically significant. There is also a theory that the name Porus was not personal but a title used for several rulers in the area, which may explain the confusion in Greek writings. To them, all the local kings might have appeared as parts of a single resistance against Alexander.

What makes Porus mysterious is how little he is mentioned in Indian sources. The Vedic hymns, the later Puranas, and the early Buddhist texts all remain silent about him. This absence has led to questions. The most frequently asked is how could a king who faced one of history's most famous conquerors vanish from local memory so completely?

Several explanations exist. One is that his region soon came under new rulers after Alexander's departure, first under the Greek governors and later under Chandragupta Maurya. As the Mauryan Empire rose, Porus's legacy may have merged into a broader story of unification rather than remaining an individual legend. Another explanation is that Indian writers of that time preferred to record continuity and moral order instead of the personal heroism that Greek historians admired. Kings were remembered not for single acts of bravery but for maintaining stability and justice within their realms.

Still, Porus endures as a figure of quiet strength. Even through Greek descriptions, he appears as a tall and dignified ruler who met Alexander not as a defeated enemy but as an equal. Whether his true name was Paurava or something that time has erased, he came to represent the courage and endurance of India itself.

Chapter 2 – The Harappan Civilization

The rivers that once witnessed the might of both Alexander and Porus still exist. For many centuries, they moved across the plains, steady and almost unchanged. While the Hydaspes and the Acesines wound their way into the great Indus, the Ravi flowed through fields and villages scattered around the Punjab plains, passing from the hills of Himachal into the heart of what is now India and Pakistan. The battles of the past had long faded, but these rivers were destined to witness yet another figure who would leave a mark on history—though this time, he was neither native to the land nor arriving for battle. His name was James Lewis, a soldier of the British East India Company, though he did not keep that name for long.

We do not know much about his early life except for the fact that he enlisted young, at the age of twenty-one. This was common back then, especially for those who sought steady pay. Unsurprisingly, the Company was strict. One of the most serious crimes was dissertation. Lewis was well aware of this, yet in 1827, he deserted his post in Agra. Why he did so remains uncertain, but many suggest he had simply had enough of the experience. Whatever the cause, once he fled, he became a wanted man.

To survive, Lewis had to create a new identity. And so, he began to introduce himself as Charles Masson. With this new name, he embarked on multiple explorations. He wore simple clothing, carried little, and kept to himself. When questioned about his origins, he changed his story with ease.

Masson knew that he could not wander forever. At some point, he would have to face the Company he had deserted. But, if he had information or discoveries valuable enough, he could bargain for a pardon—or at least a lighter punishment. And thus began his mission across the Punjab into regions once crossed by Alexander's army.

He followed the Ravi River through the countryside, arriving at sites where ancient battles had once taken place. Masson was an avid reader of classical historians, so he was well-versed in the history of the lands. He had read Arrian and Quintus Curtius. He knew the stories of the Macedonian army crossing the rivers, fighting elephants, and meeting Porus in battle. These were the very stories that fired his imagination, and he hoped to find coins, weapons, or ruins that could be linked to that famous campaign.

Masson would walk along the banks with a small notebook in hand, jotting down every detail he saw. He noted the shape of old roads, the patterns of the abandoned brickwork, and any other sign of ancient settlements—no matter how small. He imagined Alexander's soldiers marching across these same fields, looking for a place to cross the river. He knew that many British scholars admired the Greeks, and bringing back evidence connected to Alexander would surely improve his chance of securing forgiveness. But it did not happen the way he expected.

One day, while passing a small settlement near the Ravi, Masson noticed several large mounds. They looked far from natural. They stood out clearly against the surrounding plain, rising in gentle slopes of baked earth and scattered debris. From afar, they resembled nothing more than low hills. However, the closer he got, it was clear that they were built not by mother nature but by human hands.

Masson returned to these strange mounds several times in the following months, convinced they were remnants of a forgotten past. Bricks lay everywhere, though most of them were either broken or covered in thick dust. However, each was the same shape and size. Weirdly enough, only Masson thought the site was special. Villagers nearby would walk over the mounds freely, often collecting what they needed for building walls, stables, and even roads. Even the British later did the same. No one thought the mounds were a part of an ancient site; they were simply convenient sources of material.

Still convinced he was a step closer to a great discovery, Masson continued to find proof. He examined the bricks with care and searched through the surface debris for hours. Patience is indeed a virtue: Masson eventually found small objects buried in the soil, including pottery shards with smooth finishes, bits of terracotta, and pieces of painted wares. The most intriguing of all were a few tiny seals carved with animals and symbols that were completely unfamiliar to a foreigner like himself. None of them matched the Greek or Persian traditions he knew from history books.

At the time, archaeology in India was almost nonexistent. There were no formal excavations, no trained teams, and no scientific surveys like those in Europe. Much of India's ancient past was understood through classical writers who mentioned Alexander or the Persians, or through Sanskrit texts that described early kingdoms and rituals.

Masson kept detailed notes of his findings—from the dimensions of the bricks to the patterns of the exposed walls, and even the distribution of pottery fragments. His days were often filled with sorting through the seals repeatedly. Some featured a unicorn-like creature, while others had an image of a bull or rows of peculiar symbols with no obvious meaning. These notes, along with his observations, would eventually form part of his published work called the *Narrative of Various Journeys in Balochistan, Afghanistan and the Panjab.*

Baked seals belonging to the Indus civilization.'

Masson compared these findings with what he knew of the region. Upon countless hours of study, he found that the style of the artifacts had no match in known Indian history. They weren't Mauryan, Kushan, or Gupta. They were certainly not from the period of Alexander, either. Their uniformity suggested a society that used standard construction methods, something far more organized than a temporary settlement. The more he saw, the more convinced he became that the ruins belonged to a civilization far older than any known kingdom in northern India.

Masson reported his discoveries to British officials in the region, yet he received a disappointing (but not surprising) response. As usual, the colonial officers were more interested in sites connected to Greece, Rome, or Persia—the mainstream colossal forces of the ancient world. In their point of view, a forgotten city with no connection to classical texts held little, if any, value. Without inscriptions they could understand, the ruins seemed unimportant. So, the mounds remained untouched.

Masson moved on with his other explorations. Later, in 1834, his identity was almost blown when he was visiting a town in the Persian Gulf. Luckily, he managed to deceive the British authorities by claiming he was an American traveler from Kentucky who had been exploring the world for a decade. Interestingly, the authorities not only believed his false identity but also befriended him. Intelligence was precious back then, so knowing that he had been traveling, the British asked Masson to write a report detailing everything about the countries he had visited. He complied, and eventually, the authorities pieced together his real identity. However, since he provided them with valuable information from his travels, Masson was pardoned. Later, he was given funds to launch excavations and expeditions across Afghanistan and the wider frontier regions the Company sought to understand.

A part of the excavation site at Harappa.[5]

It was only decades later that the site Masson discovered was formally excavated and gained a name. It all began during the construction of the railway line between Lahore and Multan when engineers and workers noticed the large mounds and the endless supply of sturdy bricks. They initially used them to build the railway beds and stations. Only afterward did scholars realize that they had destroyed parts of the ruins Masson had first recorded. The station built nearby was called Harappa, the name that would eventually be given to the entire ancient culture.

Major excavations at Harappa began in 1921, and shortly after, archaeologists also uncovered another city known as Mohenjo Daro. These two cities were roughly five hundred kilometers apart, but both belonged to the same civilization. (Harappa is in modern-day Punjab, while Mohenjo Daro is in Sindh.) They followed the same grid pattern; their streets were typically laid out in straight lines that intersected at right angles, forming blocks much like those found in modern towns. Their main avenues were broad enough to accommodate carts and foot traffic. The smaller lanes that branched from them are believed to have led into residential areas.

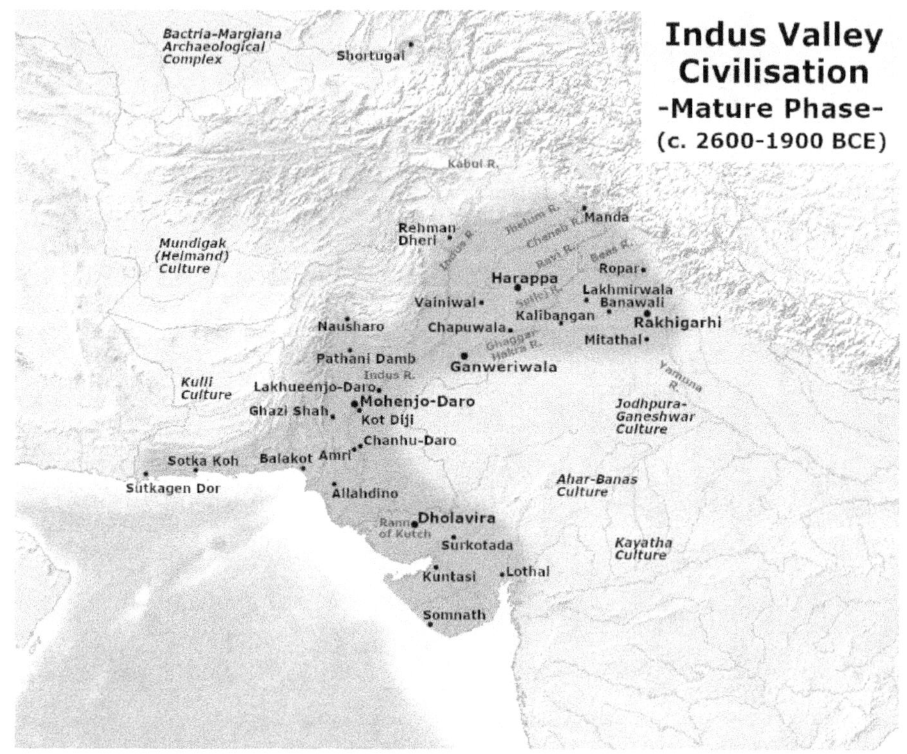

A map of the Indus Valley.[6]

Since they'd been built during the height of the Indus Valley world (c. 3000 BCE), it is not surprising that the houses were constructed with remarkable consistency. Every one of the bricks that formed the structures followed a standard size that appeared across the entire civilization—from Gujarat in the south to Punjab in the north.

However, one of the most impressive features of these cities was not the buildings themselves but the drainage system. Every house, even the smallest, was connected to a covered drain that ran beneath the streets. These drains were built with tightly fitted bricks and inspection points at regular intervals. This allowed wastewater to flow from homes into the main channels and out of the city. It is safe to say that only a few ancient civilizations gave such attention to public sanitation. Even in many modern towns, such careful planning would be considered advanced.

The excavations of public buildings in these cities also proved that the people paid attention to organized life. Harappa once had large granaries that were raised on platforms. They also featured ventilation channels to keep stored grain dry and safe. The scale suggested a system of food collection and distribution run by officials or councils. Nearby workshops possibly produced pottery, beads, and tools. Their layout indicated craft districts where artisans worked in regulated spaces rather than scattered individual huts.

Mohenjo Daro was home to one of the most remarkable structures of the ancient world, the Great Bath. This large rectangular pool was lined with finely fitted bricks, coated with a sealant to make them watertight. Stairs descended into the water from both ends, and the complex was surrounded by small rooms. While the purpose of the Great Bath is not fully known, its design suggests some form of ritual washing or controlled public gathering. About two thousand years later, Roman cities would become famous for their baths, complete with heated rooms, pools, and spaces for social life. Those baths were often places of leisure, trade, and conversation, built in marble and decorated with statues.

In comparison, the Great Bath of Mohenjo Daro was simpler in appearance. It featured no columns or mosaics. Where Roman baths projected luxury and imperial power, the Indus bath projected careful construction and shared use. It hints at a community that valued cleanliness, order, and perhaps a common ritual life, long before Rome existed.

Some scholars agree that this Indus civilization stood out for its distinctive approach—especially when compared with other ancient cultures. While the ancient Egyptians built upward, with their pyramids and obelisks that pierced the sky, Harappa preferred to build outward. This civilization created cities that stretched across the plains with careful planning and repeated patterns.

The Mesopotamia civilization was known for recording the deeds of kings and laws on clay tablets. The Indus people, however, had a different method: they carved their symbols on small seals, leaving behind scripts that mostly remain undeciphered to this day.

The Greeks loved to celebrate their heroes and legends in their art and literature, while the people of the Indus Valley left no statues of kings and heroes. Their achievements seem to speak of collective effort rather than personal glory.

Even though the civilization did not seem to glorify luxury or sophistication as much as the other popular ancient cultures, the Indus cities were not isolated. Trade connected them to the wider world.

Records from Mesopotamia mentioned a place called Meluhha. Historians and scholars alike believe they were referring to the lands of the Indus. The reason is simple. Meluhha lay beyond Magan and Dilmun, across the sea to the east, exactly where the Indus cities stood. The Mesopotamian texts also mentioned goods they obtained from Meluhha, like carnelian beads, ivory, and timber, which were all typically found in Harappan workshops. Indus-style seals and weights have also been unearthed in Mesopotamian cities, further cementing the theory that the two civilizations were in contact through long distance trade.

When systematic excavations began in the Indus Valley in the early twentieth century, one of the first major findings came from the work of Sir John Marshall. The director of the Archaeological Survey of India, Marshall had an extensive portfolio; he had already worked in Greece and the Near East. So, when he first approached the mounds of Harappa and Mohenjo Daro, he expected to find things he was familiar with. But, alongside another archaeologist, Ernest John Henry Mackay, what he uncovered was different from anything he had seen before.

Harappan weights, now stored in the National Museum of New Delhi.[7]

What stunned these men the most was how different the Indus cities were from other ancient sites already known to archaeology. Egypt had massive temples and elaborate tombs built specifically for pharaohs and his families. Mesopotamia was popular for its towering ziggurats and palaces. At those sites, authority was carved in stone and raised high above the common streets.

Marshall and Mackay expected these when they first excavated the Indus cities. But instead, as we've mentioned, Harappa and Mohenjo Daro left behind no sprawling palaces, no obvious temples, and no monuments that celebrated kings or priests. The buildings were practical, with a focus on houses, storage areas, workshops, and civic structures.

Some scholars now suggest that the absence of grand palaces or temples does not mean the absence of strong leadership. Instead, it may indicate a different kind of political structure. It's plausible that the Indus cities were governed by councils made up of merchants, landholders, and elders rather than by single rulers who displayed their authority through monuments. Power may have been expressed through consistency, planning, and control of resources rather than through statues and royal buildings.

Archaeologists even found it difficult to unearth weapons. Instead of war equipment and weapons, they only uncovered small copper knives, a few arrowheads, and tools that seemed more suited to craft work, daily tasks, and hunting. No large stores of spears or swords were ever discovered. Excavators also saw no traces of major battle, no layers of ash that mark the burning of a city, and no mass graves that serve as proof of a violent end. Although some citadel mounds existed, they lacked the heavy defensive walls and towers that characterized the fortified cities of Mesopotamia or Egypt.

If conflicts occurred, they were not turned into public monuments or detailed written records that have survived. There are no known scenes of battle, no praise poems for generals, and no reliefs showing armies in formation. It appears that this culture did not glorify war in the same way. Disputes or struggles, if they took place, may have been smaller in scale or handled within the framework of local communities and councils rather than large imperial campaigns. Here the contrast with Greece, Rome, and Mesopotamia becomes clearer. Greek and Roman cultures recorded their conflicts in detail. Writers such as Herodotus, Thucydides, Polybius, and Livy never shy away from vividly recording battles, campaigns, coups, and shifting alliances. These stories of conquests and victories were recorded not only in scrolls but also their cities' arches, columns, and temples. War was undeniably central to their identity and public memory. In Mesopotamia, kings carved their victories on stone stelae, boasted of defeated enemies, and built enormous structures that projected strength. Conflict and rulership were displayed openly and deliberately.

And so, in 1931, Marshall and Mackay concluded in their report that the people of Mohenjo Daro and other Indus cities were neither warlike nor fearful of invasion. Their view shaped the early image of the Indus Valley Civilization as a peaceful and cooperative society.

Later research, however, made this picture more complex. Modern scholars emphasize that the limited number of weapons in the Indus Valley's archaeological record does not necessarily rule out violence. Many Indus tools and objects were made from copper, wood, and other materials that decay over time. Weapons made of perishable materials would not survive thousands of years in the soil. In addition, later excavations at some sites have uncovered skeletons with injuries, including skull fractures and other trauma, which point to episodes of interpersonal violence or unrest. These remains do not suggest great wars but do show that life was not entirely free from conflict.

Environmental and social pressures were a likely source of conflict. Studies of ancient river systems show that the courses of the Indus and related rivers shifted over time. Flooding, drought, and the drying of certain channels would have threatened crops and trade. A society that depended on careful management of water and agriculture would have felt these changes sharply. Competition for land and resources could have led to disputes.

There is also evidence that some Indus cities contained elements of controlled access and protection. Citadel mounds created raised areas that were easier to defend. Gateways regulated entry into certain sectors. The grid layout of streets, while practical, also allowed movement to be watched and directed. These features suggest that the people of Harappa and Mohenjo Daro understood risk and took measures to manage it, even if they did not surround their cities with massive stone walls.

Taken together, the evidence suggests that the Indus Valley Civilization was stable and highly organized but not entirely free from tension or danger. It differed from Greece, Rome, and Mesopotamia not because it lacked conflict but because it did not celebrate or monumentalize it. Authority seems to have been quieter, spread through systems and planning rather than embodied in a single visible ruler.

Labeling the Indus Valley as a purely peaceful civilization oversimplifies reality. The people of the Indus Valley may not have sought glory through war, yet they understood power, order, and survival.

The Vanishing of the Ancient Cities

It is believed that around 1900 BCE, Harappa and Mohenjo Daro, cities once bustling with craftsmen, merchants, and traders, went through early signs of decline. Streets that had been regularly maintained began to fill with debris. Workshops fell silent. Public buildings were no longer repaired. But the change was gradual rather than sudden, and no evidence suggests that invading armies were responsible.

What remains of Mohenjo Daro.[8]

The reasons behind this decline are complex, but the largest culprit could be mother nature and time. As mentioned, studies of ancient river systems show that the Indus and its tributaries shifted their courses over time. Some rivers dried; others moved far from the cities they once supported. This unfortunate change undoubtedly threatened agriculture, which depended on the predictable cycles of flooding and irrigation. Eventually, fields that had once been fertile turned dry, making it difficult to cultivate. In some regions, signs of over-farming and soil exhaustion appear in the archaeological record.

There was a clear domino effect. With less water and failing harvests, trade networks weakened. The long-distance exchange that had once connected the Indus Valley to Mesopotamia and Central Asia began to shrink. Merchants lost the stability that had once allowed them to move goods across wide regions.

As resources thinned, people gradually left the cities in search of more reliable land. Small groups and families began moving east toward the Gangetic Plain, which offered more dependable rainfall and open areas for settlement. Of course, the movement was not an organized migration but more of a slow dispersal over many years. As people spread out, the large cities were abandoned. Brick by brick, time and weather reduced them to the mounds that Charles Masson later explored.

It is safe to assume that no single culture replaced the Indus world immediately. Instead, new patterns of life emerged in the north and east, forming the early stages of what would later become known as the Vedic age. The people who lived in the Ganges region built different kinds of settlements, used new forms of pottery, and developed new social structures. Still, it is likely that elements of the Indus tradition survived among the communities that carried the memory of the old cities with them.

The influence of the Indus Valley can be seen in the persistence of standardized weights and measures in later periods, in certain craft techniques, and possibly in symbols that appear in later religious traditions. The careful planning of Harappa and Mohenjo Daro, with their regulated streets and civic management, may have shaped later Indian ideas of order, balance, and communal responsibility. So, even without written records, the Indus world left traces in the way its towns were organized and in the value placed on collective life.

By the time the first Vedic settlements grew into chiefdoms, the Indus cities were already memories buried deep beneath earth and sand. But their foundations, both physical and cultural, helped shape the next chapters of India's story. The disappearance of this early civilization made room for the rise of new kingdoms, new beliefs, and new leaders.

Chapter 3 – Chanakya, the Key to Chandragupta's Rise

The Nanda Empire was founded by Mahapadma Nanda sometime between 345 to 340 BCE—a time when India was experiencing remarkable growth. Based in Magadha, with its capital at Pataliputra, the empire controlled some of the richest lands in the subcontinent.

The Gangetic Plain produced grain in such abundance that it could feed multiple cities and armies at once. The empire also had its hands on many mines that were full of gold and other precious stones. Trade routes connected Magadha to distant regions, allowing various goods and tributes to travel directly into its treasury. From these resources, the Nandas built what Greek writers later described as one of the largest military forces of the ancient world. They wrote of thousands of infantry and cavalry, long lines of chariots, and elephants that marched like moving towers.

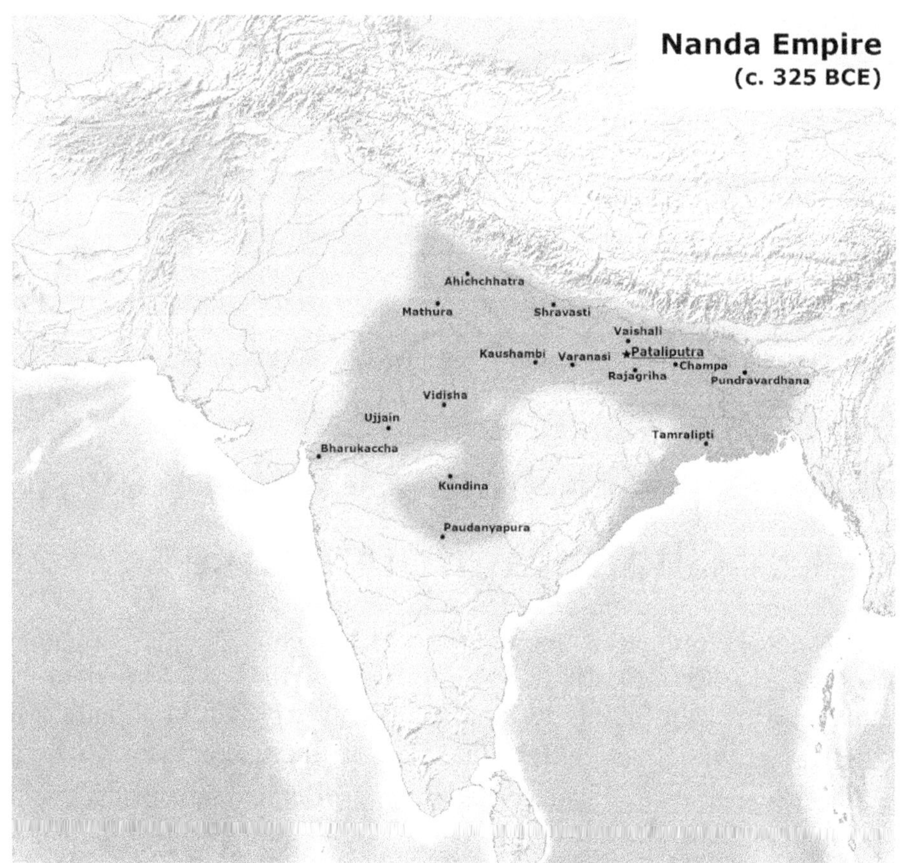

The extent of the Nanda Empire circa 325 BCE.[9]

Of course, every empire had its own set of challenges. Despite its power and wealth, there was distance between the empire's ruler and its subjects. Maintaining a colossal army had always been costly, so taxes were heavy. Farmers had to pay substantial portions of their harvests. Merchants, though still active and influential, eventually found themselves navigating through layers of officials whose duties were tied closely to taxation. And so, especially in the countryside, many local rulers and clan chiefs began to resent Magadha's authority.

As if these problems were not enough, Magadha also featured a social order that further added to the tension. Indian society had several classes, each with traditional roles in religion, warfare, trade, and labor. One of these classes was known as the Brahmins, who were long seen as the caretakers of learning and rituals. They held influence in the Nanda Empire, but that influence was not constant; it varied from court to court. Some valued their counsel, using them as guides to craft policy and custom. Others, including the Nanda court, preferred to look to administrators and military commanders, whose priorities were more practical. As a result, these scholars were not always treated with the respect they believed their learning deserved.

A Brahmin named Chanakya experienced this mistreatment firsthand. He was often described in Brahminical stories as a brilliant scholar from Taxila. He was well-versed in not only ritual and religion but also statecraft and philosophy. Another legend spoke of Chanakya being born with a complete set of teeth—a sign that the child was destined to become a king. His parents, however, knew such a path was not easy. Rather than accepting the prophecy, they were disturbed. So, they removed his teeth, hoping that Chanakya's destiny would be altered. But the astrologers were adamant that the royal destiny would not disappear.

A depiction of Chanakya.[10]

They were certain that it would pass to someone he guided instead.

And it was true: Chanakya would soon become a king maker. This particular story began when he traveled to Magadha sometime near the end of the fourth century BCE. He was expecting the reception that a scholar of his rank usually received. But things went south when the Nanda king—possibly Dhana Nanda, the son of Mahapadma Nanda—mocked him. Legend has it that it was because of the Brahmin's lack of teeth or simply his less appealing appearance. Other sources disagree with this narrative, claiming that the king never mocked him but simply dismissed him outright without listening. Whatever the exact details, this moment was a turning point that set Chanakya on a new path. Soon after, he left the court with controlled anger and a promise. From then on, he had one mission: to topple down the Nanda Empire.

Chanakya made his way toward the city of Taxila, where many roads intersected, carrying merchants, envoys, teachers, and students from all over the distant lands. Interestingly, the city had no single ruler. It thrived mostly on trade, ideas, and the movement of people. Here Chanakya remained, teaching curious minds for some time. Meanwhile, he kept his eyes open and his ears sharp, listening intently to even the smallest news about the empire.

One day, he encountered a certain boy whom he believed had potential. His name was Chandragupta Maurya. Details of his background are murky; we do not have a single confirmed origin. The Jain tradition, for one, claimed Chandragupta belonged to the Maurya tribe, which was possibly part of the ancient Kshatriya (traditional warrior class of ancient India). Others wrote that he was raised among hunters or a group of herdsmen. Whatever his origins, he does not appear in the legends as a polished figure. The stories describe a boy who was bold, curious, and quick-thinking but also rough around the edges, untrained in the formalities of royal courts.

However, Chanakya did not approach the young Chandragupta immediately. He kept a close watch on him before finally interacting with him. Their early interactions were not sentimental. Chanakya did not take him as a son or as a prodigy to admire. He saw in him something useful—potential that could be shaped into a force capable of challenging a powerful dynasty. So, their relationship, as remembered in the narratives, was built on purpose rather than affection.

From Chanakya, Chandragupta learned the basics of statecraft, warfare, and the structure of kingdoms. He was told to observe the ways rulers gain and lose support. Chanakya also bestowed on him the art of alliances. He was taught how allies were important, especially in a land divided by many clans. Chanakya tested Chandragupta's memory with stories of ancient kings, often asking the young boy to repeat the lessons in his own words. Chanakya also instilled discipline in Chandragupta, emphasizing its importance in a strong leader. Whenever the young Chandragupta acted recklessly, Chanakya would correct him. In other words, the scholar was always by his side, working to refine his natural energy into direction and strategy.

Of course, the training in Taxila was not confined to lessons and conversations. As Chandragupta absorbed his teachings, Chanakya began laying the foundation of what would become a quiet but far-reaching campaign against the Nandas. He knew that confronting Magadha head on would mean certain death. He must ensure that the empire was weakened from within before making any direct challenge. And, as if the heavens were on his side, the opportunity was laid right in front of him.

Taxila was the perfect place to gather intelligence and build alliances due to the constant movement of merchants, monks, and foreign travelers. He shared meals with travelers who had passed through border towns and listened to their stories about discontent among local chiefs. Ancient sources also describe how Chanakya would dispatch men and women across the land, disguised as wandering ascetics, storytellers, healers, and traders. Unsuspected, these spies could observe the roads and settlements. They counted the number of soldiers, took note of their rotating shifts, and eavesdropped on rumors and reports about shortages of grain. Through these wandering men and women, Chanakya learned which officials were corrupt, which governors were resented by their subjects, and which towns were holding their anger as they were abandoned by the Nanda court.

Chanakya also made use of the merchants. Long distance trade was the lifeblood of the northwest, so those who moved goods across great distances often knew more about the state of the land than any court official. He spoke with merchants who carried goods to Pataliputra and never shied away from lending his ears when they complained about taxes that ate into their profits and were reportedly high enough to discourage long journeys. So, it was relatively easy for Chanakya to convince these merchants to aid him. They were willing to cooperate if they believed there was a chance for change. Through them, Chanakya gained contacts in market towns and ports, forming an informal network of traders who could carry news faster than most messengers.

Bribery and misinformation played their part as well. Once Chanakya knew which officials in the Nanda administration could be swayed and which commanders lacked loyalty, he began scheming with the help of his coin purse. Money sent through the right channels opened doors that would otherwise have remained shut. Rumors were also spread in places where they would cause friction, and doubts were planted among those who already felt neglected by the royal court. The aim was not chaos but erosion, a slow weakening of the structure that held the empire together.

Of course, spies and the cooperation of merchants were not enough to bring down an empire. It was crucial for Chanakya to gather more concrete supporters. So, he sought allegiance with the clans that lived beyond the direct clutch of Magadha—especially those who had lost autonomy under earlier Magadhan rulers and were forced to suppress their grievances with the Nandas. Knowing that these clans were only lying low until an opportunity came, Chanakya approached them with practical agreements. He offered future influence, trade advantages, and reduced taxes if the clans agreed to support him when the time came. One of his strongest allies was Parvataka, the king of the mountain kingdom known as Himavatkuta. In exchange for his alliance, Chanakya offered him half of Nanda's empire—but would soon resort to trickery to reverse the offer.

By the time Chanakya and his protege Chandragupta left Taxila, the empire's outer regions were slowly eroding. The heart of the empire still appeared strong, but beneath the surface, cracks had begun to form. And, interestingly, these cracks were not opened by fierce soldiers and large-scale battles but by a network of ordinary people who followed the whispers of a patient scholar.

Meanwhile, the future ruler, Chandragupta, had grown into a fine, more disciplined man. Many years following his first interaction with Chanakya, he began moving with small groups of followers. True, these were not large armies that could challenge the Nandas openly. But their numbers were strong enough to strike the empire's outposts and intercept supply lines. Over time, Chandragupta's name had become known by those who longed to see the empire crumble. His growing number of supporters, combined with the stories of his feats, allowed him to encourage local rulers to turn against Magadha.

As Chanakya's efforts continued to spread unease, the Nandas found themselves increasingly isolated. Dhana Nanda, remembered in later stories as a king who cared for nothing but his own wealth and pride, began to sense the nearing danger. But, with the size of his army and the riches of his treasury, the king was confident. He was certain Chandragupta was only a small thorn in the thicket. Little did he know, armies loyal to their source of pay often lose their spirit when stability falters, and riches offer little protection when the channels that carry them are disrupted.

With the help of Parvataka, Chanakya and Chandragupta made their major move. They marched their army and laid siege to the many cities scattered close to Pataliputra. One city, whose name has been lost to time, is said to have put up strong resistance. The old story describes how Chanakya successfully tricked the city into lowering their guards. Disguised as a Shaivite mendicant (holy person), he entered the city and offered a word of advice. He suggested that the heavens had spoken that the siege would only end if the idols of the seven mothers were removed from the town's temple. The defenders, ever superstitious and perhaps driven by desperation, quickly followed his suggestion. After the idols were removed, Chanakya quietly ordered his army to end the siege. The defenders, glad to have followed the humble mendicant's words, rejoiced and began celebrating their victory. This was the time: Chanakya's army launched a surprise attack and captured the city soon after.

It was only after subduing all the regions outside the capital that Chanakya and Chandragupta moved toward Pataliputra. They captured the capital city but spared the Nanda emperor. He was allowed to escape death by going into exile, taking nothing more than a cart of goods. Some Sanskrit texts say that when the emperor and his family were leaving the city, his daughter caught a glimpse of Chandragupta and immediately fell in love. She then chose him as her husband, following a traditional practice known as *svayamvara* in which a woman chooses her spouse herself. But as she stepped down from the cart to approach the new ruler, nine spokes of the cart's wheel mysteriously broke. Chanakya saw this incident as an omen, claiming that the Maurya dynasty, beginning with Chandragupta, would last for nine generations. Whether Chandragupta married the princess remains uncertain since no historical evidence was found to support the legend.

Meanwhile, Parvataka was also said to have fallen in love with one of Nanda's *visha kanyas* (legendary female assassins in ancient India who specialized in poisoning their targets). Ancient Sanskrit writings claim that Chanakya approved of the marriage. Unfortunately, Parvataka succumbed to poison when he touched the woman during their wedding. This was the moment Chanakya saw a chance to reverse his words to Parvataka years earlier. He urged Chandragupta to not call a physician and let Parvataka die.

With Parvataka now off the chess board, Chandragupta became the sole ruler of Nanda's territories. This was the birth of the Mauryan Empire, which lasted from 321 BCE to 186 BCE.

With the regions now under a new sovereign, reconstruction soon began. Although Chandragupta sat at the top of the hierarchy, Chanakya's influence could be felt in the early years of the Mauryan Empire. Vast experiences had taught him that a kingdom built on shifting alliances needed firm roots, so meticulous changes had to be made. Perhaps to keep Chankya's word, taxes were reorganized, ensuring fairness and consistency. Next, the fresh empire appointed new administrators who were screened for their skill and reliability rather than their connection to the court. Land was measured, surveyed, and recorded so that the state could further understand its own resources.

Even Pataliputra experienced change. The city that had served many earlier dynasties soon grew into a more structured administrative center. Its channels were cleared and its roads greatly repaired. New quarters were built to accommodate the increasing number of officials, scribes, and workers. Discipline had always been the most important quality in both Chanakya and Chandragupta's eyes. So, they expected to see this quality in the empire's system of governance. Reports from distant regions must be submitted on time, and revenue collection must follow measured rules instead of fluctuating demands. To eradicate corruption—or lessen it, at least—officials who served the crown worked under closer supervision.

Trade, which had shown signs of weakening under the Nandas, began to strengthen once more. The new administration system no longer treated the merchants as convenient sources of quick revenue. Farmers, too, could breathe easier as they were freed from excessive taxes and vague regulations.

Inscriptions and later accounts speak of an empire that grew more stable with each passing year. While Chandragupta provided the authority, Chanakya supplied the framework that allowed the new emperor to manage a large and diverse land. But as this order settled across the Gangetic Plain, events unfolding far to the west began to draw closer to India's borders.

Alexander's death brought chaos. His vast empire was fractured among his four generals, who were eager to carve out a domain from the territories he had conquered. One of the four generals was known as Seleucus. This seasoned commander claimed the former Persian lands that stretched from Babylon to the foothills of the Hindu Kush. And so, when news of the new Mauryan Empire reached his ears, Seleucus started strategizing.

Seleucus marched east sometime in 305 BCE, confident that he could assert control over a valley he believed to be a part of the Macedonian inheritance. However, when he reached the borders, what he witnessed surprised him. The Mauryan Empire was undeniably strong. It was unified and organized, complete with a massive army. This was far from the fragile, scattered territory he had expected. Historians wrote that war took place, but only for a short while. Details are unclear, but Chandragupta eventually proved that the Mauryan Empire was not to be trifled with. Continuing the war would be unwise, so Seleucus chose to make a treaty with Chandragupta.

Through this treaty, they established diplomatic relations. Seleucus agreed to leave several eastern provinces (including the areas of modern Afghanistan and Pakistan) firmly in the hands of Chandragupta. In return, the Mauryan Empire gifted Seleucus with five hundred war elephants, which later became a major asset in Hellenistic warfare. These very elephants accompanied Seleucus in the Battle of Ipsus (301 BCE), in which he emerged victorious.

With peace achieved and another major conflict evaded, Seleucus sent Megasthenes to Pataliputra as an ambassador. His observations of the foreign lands, later compiled in *Indica*, introduced the Greek world to Indian cities, customs, and political organization. Through him, information traveled in both directions, creating one of the earliest formal links between the Mauryan state and the Mediterranean world.

As the empire strengthened its ties abroad, life within the court moved steadily into a new generation. Chandragupta's reign, shaped so deeply by Chanakya's guidance, was approaching its middle years when stories surrounding the birth of his son began to take form. These stories come from much later sources, yet they became some of the most widely repeated tales in Indian tradition.

Chanakya was determined to protect the king from poison, a common danger in ancient courts. It was believed that Chanakya would quietly add small amounts of poison to the king's meals to build immunity. But this resulted in a tragedy one day when the Mauryan emperor shared his meal with his pregnant queen. While Chandragupta could withstand the poison, a single bite was all it took for the queen to collapse to the floor. Chanakya, realizing what had happened, rushed to the queen's side. It was too late for the queen—but not her unborn child. Legend has it that Chanakya cut open the queen's womb and rescued the baby before the poison could spread further. However, a single drop managed to touch the child's forehead, leaving behind a dark mark. Apart from this permanent mark, the boy was unharmed. This drop of poison led to his name, Bindusara, which means "the strength of the drop."

As for Chandragupta, he did not remain on the throne until his death. Later traditions suggest that he withdrew from public life and surrounded himself with the teachings of Jain monks. In 298 BCE, he abdicated the throne and made a journey south to Karnataka. There, he lived the remainder of his life as an ascetic. Jain traditions also say that the former emperor later undertook a ritual fast to death.

Meanwhile, in Pataliputra, the matters of governance were left to his son, Bindusara, whose rise marked the second generation of Mauryan rule (out of nine). Mirroring his father before him, Bindusara was a capable ruler. He maintained the vast territories once secured by Chandragupta and built on the disciplined system that had been established. His reign is remembered as a time of stability. Relations with Hellenistic kingdoms continued, and the Mauryan court retained its reputation as a center of order and intelligence. Envoys traveled between India and the western realms, carrying messages, gifts, and news. And through all of this, Chanakya continued to work behind the scenes, advising the young king and ensuring that the structures of governance remained intact.

The ruins of Pataliputra.[11]

However, Chanakya's time was almost up. Many historians agree that he died in 275 BCE, but they are uncertain about the manner of his death. Some records say that political tension began to take place within the court. Bindusara is said to have shunned the old Chanakya after listening to an accusation made by a courtier named Subandhu. The courtier, jealous of the advisor and wishing to remove him from power, told the emperor about his mother's death, whispering that Chanakya purposely poisoned the queen.

Driven by anger, Bindusara dismissed Chanakya, who went on to live quietly in a forest. But Subandhu still could not rest easy; he was afraid that Chanakya would soon plan his return. So, he arranged for the humble hut where Chanakya was staying to be burned to ashes. His plan worked, and the ninety-two-year-old Chanakya died. Bindusara eventually regretted his decision. He arranged for a reconciliation, but all was too late.

Chapter 4 – Ashoka's Unique Transformation

Being good is not easy. And trying to uphold benevolence while at the top of the hierarchy is even harder. Wearing a crown unsurprisingly comes with a myriad of responsibilities: managing lands and taxes, commanding armies, judging disputes, punishing treason, settling succession, holding fragile coalitions together, and determining the fate of thousands with a single decision. Absolute power also amplifies impulses. Fear could easily turn into extreme paranoia, caution into blind suspicion, and discipline into cruelty. Even a well-intentioned king could slip into brutality when put under pressure.

History has endless pages that illustrate this pattern. In China, the first emperor, Qin Shi Huang, was credited with unifying the warring states. But alongside this contribution to civilization, he also went down in history for harsh legalism, mass executions, and (allegedly) the burning of books. It is safe to say that his achievements and his violence are inseparable in historical memory.

Mesopotamia had rulers such as Naram-Sin of Akkad who embraced divine kingship, invoking their heavenly mandate while suppressing revolts with overwhelming force. Their absolute authority justified absolute retaliation. The famous Persian king Cambyses II was also a favorite subject of discussion among Greek writers. They often described him as a cruel and unstable ruler who never hesitated to destroy anything that lay in his path to victory—though these accounts were likely exaggerated by his enemies. And Rome, too, was put under the leadership of notorious emperors many times across history. Nero, Caligula, and Caracalla were said to have been extremely paranoid, constantly thinking about their own assassinations.

Ancient traditions tended to remember rulers in extremes. Everyone was either a heroic conqueror or a monstrous tyrant—nothing in between. Only a few kings remained in the gray area. The combination of immense power, constant threats, and the need to validate authority pushed many leaders toward decisions that later generations judged harshly. And it was rare for kings to grow gentler as they aged. Often, they tightened control, punished dissent more heavily, and relied increasingly on fear to stabilize their rule.

The same, however, cannot be said of the third emperor of the Mauryan Empire, Ashoka. Admittedly, his early reputation fits perfectly alongside the names of other harsh figures of antiquity. Later Buddhist texts even referred to him as "Chandashoka," which simply means "Ashoka the Cruel." But interestingly, his story does not follow the usual arc. Instead of being remembered for increasing ruthlessness in the later years of his reign, Ashoka eventually became known as the emperor who transformed for the better.

The Violent Path to the Throne

The Mauryan Empire had grown tremendously under Chandragupta and Bindusara, but it was also politically complex. Succession within such a huge state was rarely smooth, and Ashoka's ascent became one of the most brutal episodes preserved in India's historical memory.

Ashoka was not the next in line. The designated heir was his older brother, Crown Prince Susima. Although both held significant influence in court—Susima was backed by important nobles, and Ashoka's military capabilities were acknowledged—Ashoka's unstable temper made him inferior to his brother. He was respected but at the same time feared.

Still, Ashoka would not accept defeat. Buddhist sources such as *Ashokavadana* and *Divyāvadāna* claim that a violent struggle ensued after Bindusara's passing. According to these writings, Ashoka did not hold back. He is said to have killed ninety-nine of his brothers, which was almost every rival who stood in his path.

Of course, modern historians view these numbers with skepticism. The number ninety-nine is typically used to emphasize dramatic moral transformation rather than literal events. Buddhist authors purposely wrote their narratives this way to portray Ashoka as a man who sank deeply into violence before rising into virtue. But still, their exaggeration was not baseless. The Mauryan succession was contested, and bloodshed was not uncommon in ancient royal households. Eliminating rivals—be it brothers, cousins, or influential ministers who had served the court for decades—was always a real possibility in the struggle for power. Whether Ashoka killed dozens or only a few, the underlying truth is that his ascent was marked by force and violence.

A depiction of Ashoka riding his chariot, carved on the Sanchi Stupa.[19]

Once the throne was his, the new Mauryan emperor moved quickly to consolidate his power. This was the period when his ruthless side took over almost completely. He imposed strict governance, demanding absolute obedience from both officials and commoners. Multiple traditions portray him as an autocratic ruler whose early decisions were often shaped by a combination of suspicion and a desire to assert complete control. Although few administrative details from this period survive in inscriptions, later accounts suggest he was harsh with dissenters and swift in meting out punishment to those who defied imperial authority.

One of the most infamous stories that details his brutality was recorded in the *Ashokavadana*. The story says Ashoka once ordered the massacre of 18,000 wandering ascetics in Bengal. These people were Ajivikas, a sect considered heretics by the orthodox Vedic traditions of ancient India.

Of course, as with many dramatic ancient stories, this episode must be approached with caution. Interestingly, the massacre does not appear in any contemporary inscription. Even the number—18,000—is suspiciously rounded, a typical feature of ancient storytelling. Scholars see this story as an example of polemical literature. It was designed to portray Ashoka as a zealous king who punished rival faiths and to explain the decline of the Ajivika sect.

Ashoka's Legends of Cruelty

This massacre was not the only legend preserved by Buddhist authors to frame Ashoka's life as a dramatic journey from brutality to moral awakening. While the legends' historicity is doubtful, their place in the tradition is significant, revealing how later storytellers understood and reshaped the image of the emperor.

The most memorable and daunting of all is the story of "Ashoka's Hell." This account speaks of Ashoka, said to be a sadistic ruler, building an elaborate torture chamber. Before launching the construction project, Ashoka dispatched his men across the empire with the task of finding a suitable man to become the empire's official executioner. Ashoka's men eventually found the perfect candidate, who went by the name of Girika. He was so vicious that when his parents tried to stop him from taking the position, Girika mercilessly murdered them. This was perhaps viewed as loyalty by the emperor, who swiftly appointed him as the empire's official executioner.

The executioner advised the emperor to build the torture chamber based on the suffering endured by people reborn in Buddhist hell. Ancient texts described the structure in full detail. It had a rather deceptive exterior. To those unaware of the purpose of the building, it appeared pleasing in the eyes. Its entrance was indistinguishable from that of a well-kept palace building. This beauty, however, ended at the gate.

Inside, there were horrors modeled on the five torments of Buddhist hell. The interior was said to contain boiling pits for immersing prisoners, heated metal floors meant to scorch anyone who stepped inside, hidden blades, and other violent contraptions meant to prolong suffering. Some versions add that Ashoka decreed that anyone who entered the building, whether prisoner or visitor, would never leave alive—including himself.

Weirdly enough, none of these details about the chamber appear in Ashoka's inscriptions. Scholars have also unearthed no archaeological evidence that could prove the existence of this torture complex. So, many scholars have deduced that the torture chamber was nothing more than a moral allegory—a literary device designed to represent the cruelty that Buddhist storytellers believed characterized Ashoka's early rule.

Another legend written in the *Divyāvadāna* emphasizes that Ashoka's cruelty revolved around his officials. This episode began with Ashoka assembling his ministers and ordering them to do something rather peculiar. He told them to cut down every flowering and fruit-bearing tree in the royal gardens, leaving only the trees full of thorns.

Baffled, the ministers responded with utter silence at first. Flowering trees provided shade, color, and fruit. Thorny trees, on the other hand, had no benefits and were considered nuisances. Unsure of the rationale behind their emperor's orders, the ministers approached him to seek clarification. According to ancient sources, they asked Ashoka not once but three times, hoping for an explanation or perhaps permission to disregard the command. Ashoka, however, interpreted their repeated questioning as insubordination. In a fit of rage, the emperor unsheathed his sword and beheaded five hundred of his ministers.

As with the story of the torture chamber, the details here are also far from historical. Scholars also point at the rounded number—five hundred—which was a symbolic figure commonly used in ancient storytelling. The lack of Mauryan-era sources also cements the conclusion that this episode was created by later Buddhist authors to shape readers' imagination about how Ashoka reigned in his early years. The flower trees could have represented prosperity, beauty, and generosity, while the thorny trees could have symbolized severity and harm. The emperor's preference for thorns over blossoms could be a metaphor for his moral state, and his violent reaction to questioning reflects a ruler whose authority rested on fear rather than respect.

The Transformation

All these stories, taken literally, describe a tyrant of almost theatrical cruelty. By portraying Ashoka at his worst, the storytellers create the foundation for one of antiquity's most extraordinary reversals. The greater the cruelty attributed to Chandashoka, the more astonishing the emergence of Dhammashoka appears in the narrative arc that follows.

The incident that led to his reversal varies depending on the source. One lesser-known narrative speaks of the involvement of a monk named Samudra. According to the story, Samudra was seized by Girika and imprisoned in the infamous torture chamber. There, the monk was subjected to many kinds of unthinkable punishments. Girika himself inflicted various torments on him, yet the monk remained mysteriously unscathed.

When Ashoka heard of this event, he made haste to see the monk in person. The story goes that, during their meeting, the monk directly rebuked Ashoka, speaking without fear, and confronted him with the suffering his rule had unleashed. The rebuke struck Ashoka hard enough to break through whatever indifference or cruelty had previously guided him. Samudra's admonition included the instruction to build stupas (sacred Buddhist monuments) across the empire and to ensure the protection of all living beings. The tale concludes with Ashoka burning the torture chamber to the ground. He then burned the merciless Girika to death and vowed to rule with righteousness instead of violence from then on.

In this narrative, Ashoka's transformation is instantaneous, triggered by the authority of a holy man. Whether or not such an event occurred, the story reflects a long-standing attempt to explain how someone remembered for cruelty could alter his life so dramatically.

The second version of the story, however, is more historically grounded. According to this version, Ashoka's transformation for the better was triggered by neither the acts of a holy man nor a magical incident. The emperor began to change his rule at the end of the Kalinga War.

Kalinga was once a prosperous coastal state with a strong tradition of independence. For a long time, it resisted Mauryan expansion, refusing to bid its independence goodbye. But when Ashoka launched an invasion around 260 BCE, Kalinga was forced to go through a period of terrible chaos. The campaign eventually ended in a decisive Mauryan victory. But what distinguishes this war from countless others in ancient history is the emperor's own testimony about its aftermath.

According to Ashoka's later reflections, the fighting resulted in an unimaginable loss of life. He records that approximately 100,000 people died. Another 150,000 were taken captive or deported. Many more perished from famine, displacement, and disease in the chaos that followed.

Ashoka reportedly visited the affected regions after the campaign ended. The burned settlements, scattered corpses, and sight of countless families grieving the death of their loved ones stirred his stony heart. His later reflections describe a moment when the enormity of the destruction overcame him, and remorse seized his mind with a force he had not expected.

From this experience, an internal shift began to take place. Ashoka didn't merely regret the cost of the war in administrative terms, nor did he frame it as a political miscalculation. Interestingly, the language, preserved in various forms, expresses a more personal sense of sorrow. He realized that the conquest had brought grief rather than glory and that the human cost far exceeded any strategic benefit. It is this emotional and moral turning point—not a miraculous intervention or a political necessity—that many historians view as the genuine beginning of his transformation.

Whatever mixture of personal guilt, ethical awakening, or pragmatic realization shaped Ashoka at this moment, it marked a clear departure from his earlier reputation. The emperor once remembered for eliminating his rivals without thinking twice, enforcing harsh punishments, and allowing (or at least accepting) the violence of conquest now felt the consequences of his own actions. The transformation did not require external miracles or symbolic stories; it emerged from the confrontation between his authority and the suffering that authority had produced.

The Benevolent Emperor's Policies

Ashoka's transformation did not remain an internal turning point. Over the years that followed, it reshaped the principles by which he governed. This gave rise to what later tradition called Dhammashoka, "Ashoka of Dhamma." The word "dhamma" in this context did not refer to a strictly Buddhist doctrine, nor was it a religious code meant for monks. Ashoka used it to describe a practical moral policy for the empire. This was a code of conduct that emphasized compassion, restraint, fairness in justice, and mutual respect among different social and religious groups. It was a guiding principle intended for everyone—ordinary people, officials, and even the royal household.

In the emperor's new point of view, justice required three simple things: moderation, patience, and avoiding unnecessary harshness. To ensure these ideals were put into practice, Ashoka reshuffled his administrative machinery. He appointed groups of officers he referred to as *dhamma-mahamattas*. Their duty was straightforward: they must promote moral welfare across the empire. These officials were expected to travel from province to province, keeping their eyes open for disputes and other conflicts that could result in violence if left unchecked. They advised on proper conduct and ensured that vulnerable groups, particularly the poor, the elderly, and those without family support, were not neglected. Some would say the creation of this position was one of the biggest signs of the empire's departure from conventional ancient statecraft. Instead of dedicating administrative resources to collecting taxes or suppressing never-ending rebellion, Ashoka used them to advocate for ethical behavior.

Ashoka's reforms also extended to areas that earlier rulers rarely addressed. He ordered a reduction in animal slaughter, particularly in royal kitchens, and encouraged alternatives to killing for food or ritual. He supported planting trees along roadsides, digging wells for travelers and villagers, and establishing rest houses for people journeying across the vast Mauryan territories. True, these measures might seem minor, but they reflected a broader principle: governance should strive not only to maintain order but also to ease hardship and improve the daily lives of the people who depended on it.

One of the most distinctive features of Ashoka's dhamma policy was his religious tolerance. Although he personally favored Buddhism after his transformation, the emperor refrained from imposing his beliefs on his subjects. Several of his inscriptions repeatedly emphasize that respect should be shown to all religious sects. He warned against boasting of one's own faith while disparaging another's, insisting that such behavior caused harm and hindered mutual understanding. This deliberate promotion of cross-sect dialogue was unusual in a world where religious competition often shaped political allegiance. For Ashoka, harmony among diverse traditions was a political necessity and a moral imperative.

The Dhauli Major Rock Inscription of Ashoka, with its front shaped like an elephant head.[18]

Despite this emphasis on tolerance, Ashoka's patronage played a significant role in the spread of Buddhism. He supported monastic institutions, encouraged the settlement of monks in different parts of the empire, and is traditionally associated with the convening of the Third Buddhist Council. According to later sources, the council sought to purify the monastic community by removing doctrinal disagreements and reinforcing discipline. Whether or not Ashoka directly sponsored such a council, his reign undeniably strengthened the position of Buddhism in the subcontinent.

The most far-reaching effect of his patronage was the dispatch of Buddhist envoys to regions beyond the Mauryan realm. Traditional accounts describe missions being sent to Sri Lanka, the Himalayan regions, Central Asia, and even to faraway lands under Hellenistic influence. These missions helped establish Buddhist communities abroad, laying foundations for the religion's long-term expansion. In India itself, Ashoka supported the construction of stupas and monasteries, many of which became important centers of learning and pilgrimage long after his death.

For several decades, Ashoka's efforts reshaped both the moral and religious landscape of the Mauryan Empire. Of course, it's impossible to know whether every ideal was fully implemented. But his inscriptions and administrative changes reflect a ruler who consciously attempted to reshape imperial authority through principles rarely associated with ancient monarchs.

Ashoka died sometime in 232 BCE. Despite leaving behind an empire that was still intact, his successors did not share the same moral vision. The empire bid farewell to the stability that Ashoka had maintained. Succession disputes emerged almost immediately, as different factions supported different heirs. In a vast empire that depended on strong central leadership, uncertainty at the top encouraged provincial governors to assert increasing autonomy. Some territories, especially in the south and borderlands, drifted toward practical independence, maintaining only nominal allegiance to the center. External threats soon manifested and grew too big to curb following the reign of Dasharatha (the grandson of Ashoka and the fourth Mauryan emperor).

This political decline had significant consequences for Buddhism. Regional rulers who emerged in former Mauryan territories did not inherit Ashoka's personal commitment to Buddhism. Many belonged to communities aligned with older Brahmanical traditions. As they established or revived their courts, they naturally promoted the religious practices and institutions familiar to their own lineages.

Without state sponsorship, Buddhism's position in the subcontinent changed, though it did not vanish immediately. Its influence gradually receded from the heartlands where Ashoka had once elevated it. Monasteries eventually lost royal funding, missionary activity slowed, and the religion's intellectual centers faced increasing competition from resurgent Brahmanical schools.

Over time, Buddhism became more prominent in the northwest and in regions connected to trade routes, even as it diminished in the Gangetic Plain. Meanwhile, the missions associated with Ashoka's patronage had taken root abroad, helping Buddhist thought spread to regions where it would endure long after it faded from much of India.

The enduring impact of Ashoka's transformation lies not only in his personal shift but in the scale at which he attempted to implement it. The memory of Ashoka's transformation was immortalized, shaping how later generations understood the possibilities and limits of power guided by conscience.

Chapter 5 – What Goes Around Comes Around

At a glance, life in the royal courts of the ancient world might seem like a dream without worries. Luxury and power were both included in the package, but so was danger. These royal courts were where power shifted, often without clear warning. In some halls, the change came with a shout, while in others, it emerged in complete silence—at times carried out by the very hands that once swore loyalty.

Rome, for one, knew this game too well. Several of its emperors met their fate at the hands of the Praetorian Guard, the ones ironically responsible for keeping them safe at all costs. Persia also watched its kings fall, not to foreign invasions but to generals who called themselves Persian. Even the old kingdoms of the Nile once witnessed episodes in which the pharaohs succumbed to the plots of their own attendants or viziers.

Of course, scenes like these were not confined to the western world. In the far east, across the plains of northern India, the courts of Magadha carried their own history of sudden turns. The walls of Pataliputra, no matter how high, could not completely defend its rulers against the dangers within.

One such story from this subcontinent took place in the late sixth century BCE, long before the rise of the Mauryan Empire. It was a time when the kingdom of Magadha was run by its first major ruling house, the Haryanka dynasty.

The King Killed by His Own Flesh and Blood

The throne belonged to King Bimbisara, whose reputation was pristine; he was considered one of the most respected rulers of his age. His court was known for its steady administration, and the king himself was often praised for his ability to manage alliances without constant warfare. To this day, Bimbisara is remembered for many contributions, especially annexing the kingdom of Anga to the east, which set the foundation for the rise of the Mauryan Empire. He was also believed to have been a stout protector of Buddhism. (Bimbisara was the king who built Rajagriha, a city often mentioned in Buddhist writings.)

But despite ruling the kingdom for over five decades, the king was never free from silent threats from his own court. The crown prince, Ajatashatru, had grown restless as he watched his father's long and stable reign. Some nobles and advisors in the court spread the rumor that Bimbisara favored his younger son, while others whispered to the crown prince that it was high time he claimed the crown. They pledged their loyalty to Ajatashatru not because they believed in his potential but because they hoped to increase their own power through the prince. And so, bit by bit, bigger ambition took root. Ajatashatru began to see his father as an obstacle.

Bimbisara was so focused on the kingdom that he did not fully sense the change in his son. Tension in the palace grew quietly. When the prince finally reached the point of no return—knowing he had steady support from certain court factions—he seized control of the palace guards and confronted his father. The crown prince held the king under arrest at first. He is believed to have been confined in a chamber away from the court. Only then did Ajatashatru murder him. His cause of death, however, remains a subject of debate. While some say he was starved, others say he died of shock after being tortured.

The ruins of a prison in Rajgir, believed to be the one that held King Bimbisara.[14]

Ajatashatru took the throne soon after, sometime around 492 BCE. The act that placed him there remained unspoken in public, but it shaped the atmosphere of the court. Regardless of what had happened, the new king was determined to expand Magadha's power. While Bimbisara had favored alliance and negotiation, Ajatashatru preferred to rely on military strength. He became one of the most forceful rulers of his time, launching campaigns that changed the political map of northern India. He went to war with the kingdom of Kosala, fought the powerful Licchavi confederacy, and built impressive fortifications to protect Magadha's borders. His ambition pushed the kingdom outward in every direction.

Ajatashatru reigned for about thirty-two years. However, when it was clear that the calm unity of Bimbisara's time had never fully returned, the court advisors' view of the king began to shift. Other powerful nobles soon followed suit, aligning themselves with factions rather than the throne. Ajatashatru ruled with determination, but the bond between the royal family and the court had been weakened by the act that gave him the crown.

Around 460 BCE, the king's son, Udayin, turned against him. With the support of factions within the palace, Udayin struck down his father and seized the throne. The pattern that had begun with Bimbisara repeated almost exactly, as if the palace itself had grown accustomed to resolving succession through the bloody removal of the king.

Unfortunately, after Ajatashatru's death, Magadha went through a period of decline. There were rapid changes in leadership. Udayin was later killed by a minister, and the kings who followed him ruled only briefly. Some reigned for a few years, others for only months, and many met their end through the same quiet violence that had claimed their predecessors.

Pushyamitra's Rise after Bloodshed

As you may remember, a short while after Chandragupta Maurya rose to the throne around 322 BCE, Chanakya predicted that the dynasty would last for nine generations. This was neither a curse nor a blessing—merely a statement made by a man who understood deeply how quickly loyalty could shift in the royal palace. And as the years passed, his words seemed to come truth.

After Ashoka's long reign, the throne was passed to Dasharatha. He inherited a vast realm, and keeping such an empire under complete control was never easy. His rule covered regions that still carried the Mauryan name, but it was clear that each province moved at its own pace. Southern territories became more distant, western satraps hesitated over tribute, and even the military had slowly lost the discipline that had defined the days of Chandragupta.

After Dasharatha, the empire was ruled by Samprati, who attempted his best to restore order. Some ancient sources describe how he traveled across regions, hoping he could mend strained alliances and unite the people. However, a king could only do so much; the realm he governed was no longer the mighty empire of earlier times. Skirmishes and conflicts among frontier clans became more common, and the governors entrusted to keep order often acted more on their own judgment than on instructions from Pataliputra. Although trade still resumed, enriching the empire, there were clear changes. The roads, once patrolled by loyal officials, began to see more local toll collectors and self-appointed guardians. Eventually, the empire had trouble maintaining its far-flung provinces.

During this period of decline, Brihadratha came to the throne. His authority extended over Magadha and nearby regions, but beyond that, obedience depended on negotiation rather than command. But, as the ninth emperor of the Mauryan Empire, Brihadratha was not planning to sit still as his realm collapsed around him. He spent long hours surrounded by advisors as he studied reports that came from distant towns and held audiences to reassure both nobles and common citizens that the empire was standing firm.

It's unfair to label Brihadratha a weak ruler, as it is clear he was in a difficult position. His court was divided into groups that cooperated only when necessary. Senior ministers who once served under his predecessors still carried influence, but they were more cautious than loyal. They could easily shift their loyalty, siding especially with those who seemed capable of protecting their interests. Messages sent to distant provinces returned slowly or not at all, and Brihadratha often found himself making decisions without knowing whether his orders would be respected.

Brihadratha tried all means to mend these fractures. He offered gestures of reconciliation to rival court factions and attempted to strengthen ties with regional leaders through marriage alliances and diplomatic exchanges. But each effort met with only partial success. Some nobles accepted his authority, but their concern that the empire would soon crumble never left their thoughts. Others respected him but doubted whether the Mauryan name still carried enough weight to keep the realm steady.

Even the army, once the strongest pillar of the empire, reflected the same uncertainty. The soldiers acknowledged Brihadratha's rule but preferred to look to their commanders for direction. After all, their pay was no longer as regular as before, and supplies often arrived late. Officers disagreed about priorities: whether to defend the weakening western frontier, assist local disputes in the east, or hold position and wait for clearer instructions. The soldiers felt the shift and naturally responded only to leaders who were decisive.

Brihadratha was well aware of this; he knew that it was the army that gave order to the empire. This was the reason he placed great trust in a general named Pushyamitra.

Born into a Brahmin family known for learning and strict practice, Pushyamitra chose to become a soldier early in his life. After years of disciplined service, he rose through the ranks and became a commander who valued clarity and structure—the two qualities he carried into every unit he led. When he took charge of a unit, he began with simple measures that everyone in the camp noticed. Reports were to be written and delivered at fixed times rather than whenever an officer remembered. Orders were given in plain language, repeated until even the last line in the formation understood them. When confusion broke out at a frontier post over who was responsible for supplies, he redrew the chain of command and named a single officer in charge, making it clear who answered for what. These were not dramatic reforms, but they turned scattered groups of soldiers into a force that could move as one when needed.

So, it is not surprising that the soldiers respected him. They had served under kings who once commanded absolute obedience, but they could sense that Brihadratha lacked confidence. In contrast, Pushyamitra stood before them with certainty.

However, Brihadratha saw this as a blessing. With the court no longer united and the trust of regional leaders gradually faltering, the emperor valued Pushyamitra's steady presence. Pushyamitra became his sole hope, often summoned for counsel and suggestions. Even when Brihadratha had to attend official ceremonies, he wanted Pushyamitra at his side. The Mauryan emperor knew that the public held the general in high regard but failed to notice that the soldiers' respect and loyalty ended with the general.

As the years passed, the empire moved closer to imminent ruin. There were growing dangers at the borders. The northwestern frontier, in particular, never stopped facing pressure from ambitious local powers. For many years, the Indo-Greek kingdoms had also been causing trouble there. Kings like Demetrius and Menander had been taking advantage of the weakening state of the Mauryan Empire. Some ancient writers blamed Brihadratha, who showed no signs of resistance. Because of this, the enemy managed to push through Punjab and Mathura, eventually laying attacks on Saket and Pataliputra.

Pushyamitra became convinced there was nothing the emperor could do to save his world. The only solution was to eradicate the ruler he deemed incapable and place himself on the throne. After all, he knew he had the ultimate support of his men. Brihadratha, however, remained oblivious; he strongly believed that Pushyamitra stood behind him.

One day, Brihadratha decided to hold a grand parade of the army. Historians generally agree that he held this occasion simply as a display of confidence, to show the public that the Mauryan throne still held authority and that the soldiers still marched under the royal banner. Officials welcomed the idea, and court officers accepted the invitation politely. While the army obeyed the announcement, their quiet glances clearly revealed where their respect had settled.

This was the last day the people of Magadha ever saw their emperor well and alive. At first, the parade seemed like just another grand royal celebration. The parade ground stretched wide, packed with long lines of infantry, archers, and cavalry. Elephants stood at the edges, with their keepers guiding them into position. The loud rhythm of drums could be heard across the field as the units arranged themselves in perfect rows. The banners of the Mauryan Empire proudly fluttered above them. However, even before the ceremony began, many soldiers looked not toward the royal pavilion but toward Pushyamitra, who inspected the formation with his sharp gaze.

The emperor entered last, riding in a chariot. Some say he wore no excessive decoration, choosing to appear steady and humble rather than grand. As he stepped down, attendants parted the way, and the murmur of his arrival moved through the ranks. He walked along the front lines, greeting commanders with confidence and offering brief acknowledgments to the troops. To untrained eyes, his posture carried dignity, but those who paid attention could see the strain behind it.

Pushyamitra followed a short distance behind, neither too close nor too far. He wore formal armor polished to a dull shine, his sword at his side. Those who knew him recognized the calm focus in his movements as he approached the king, ready to continue the ceremonial inspection that followed every such occasion.

When Brihadratha signaled for him to come forward, Pushyamitra stepped ahead, confident and obedient. To the spectators, it seemed like nothing more than the usual exchange between the king and his most trusted commander-in-chief. The soldiers watched in silence, accustomed to seeing the two men stand side by side during official events. The court officials who were gathering at the edge of the field also observed the interaction, unaware of what would unfold just a few moments later.

The general bowed in the expected manner, and Brihadratha leaned slightly forward, prepared to hear whatever report or respectful greeting Pushyamitra was about to deliver. In that moment of closeness, before any words were spoken, Pushyamitra unsheathed his sword. Brihadratha saw his movement, but it all happened so quickly that he failed to react in time. Without hesitance, Pushyamitra plunged his weapon straight into the ruler whose trust in him was as deep as the vast ocean. Brihadratha staggered. Perhaps shock overtook him before pain did. His attendants shouted, but none reached him in time.

Brihadratha's lifeless body collapsed to the ground, but Pushyamitra did not move a muscle. He did not attempt to flee or defend himself for the bloody act he had committed. Instead, he stood upright, still clutching his sword in one of his hands, as if he had simply accomplished a kill on the battlefield. The parade ground fell into a long, terrible stillness. Thousands of soldiers watched their emperor fall at the hands of his own commander, yet not a single rank broke formation. Not an arrow was drawn. Not a spear shifted. Some looked uneasy; others stunned, but none stepped forward to challenge the man who had led them through years of decline. The grim silence was the clearest sign of how far the empire had slipped from its old foundations. It seemed as if they accepted the death of the last Mauryan emperor with an open heart.

Brihadratha's body was carried away, and Pushyamitra immediately shouted commands to secure the palace and prevent confusion in the city. The troops obeyed at once. No riot or resistance broke throughout the empire. By the end of the day, the gates of Pataliputra opened for the general who had become the new ruler of Magadha. Just as Chanakya had predicted, the Mauryan dynasty ended with the death of Brihadratha in 185 BCE, the ninth generation.

Pushyamitra moved quickly once he entered the palace. He knew all too well that assassinating the incapable king was only the beginning. A new ruler needed soldiers who would obey his instructions, nobles who would cooperate without question, and administrators who would carry out orders without hesitation. Therefore, his first few moves were to consolidate his standings in Pataliputra.

To officially assert his authority in the eyes of both nobles and rival kings, the new emperor undertook the Ashvamedha, one of the most important Vedic royal rituals of ancient India. The rite involved a sacred horse, which was handpicked by Pushyamitra. He then released the horse to wander freely for a full year. Any king who stopped it had to fight the royal army. In Pushyamitra's case, the horse was left completely unharmed and returned to him safe and sound—showing that his authority was unchallenged. To end the ritual, he sacrificed the horse during a major ceremony that included feasting.

Then, Pushyamitra focused on restoring discipline within the army. Pushyamitra placed trusted officers in charge of key units, refreshed the chain of command, and ensured that supplies finally reached distant posts on time. The soldiers responded immediately. They had followed him while he served as general and continued to do so now that he stood at the center of authority.

One of his biggest challenges was the threat imposed by the Indo-Greek rulers. Now that Pushyamitra was at the forefront of the empire, it was time to retaliate. Headstrong as ever, the new ruler of Magadha refused to let the borders crumble any further. So, without hesitation, he sent detachments to reinforce the western regions and counter-attacked the threats laid by the Indo-Greeks. He even personally coordinated the movement of larger forces from the center of the kingdom. The conflicts that followed were violent, but they did not expand into extended campaigns. Pushyamitra pushed back the Indo-Greek advances and reminded neighboring states that Magadha still possessed strength.

Apart from issues on the border, Pushyamitra also focused his attention inward toward older practices he believed would help his efforts to stabilize the kingdom. He revived Vedic rituals that had been less prominent during the later Mauryan years. These ceremonies involved Brahmin priests, generous gifts, and the recitation of ancient verses. However, not everyone viewed this revival positively. Several Buddhist texts, particularly those written generations after Pushyamitra's rule, describe him in a more negative light. They speak of his harsh decisions: Pushyamitra allegedly destroyed monasteries and ordered the executions of many monks. Some accounts describe his raids on Buddhist centers and how he often offered rewards for killing Buddhist monks.

These accounts, however, are not completely reliable. Later historians, especially, have debated these claims. While some believe these stories mirror the real conflicts between religious communities at that time, others argue that they were shaped by later political tensions rather than the events of Pushyamitra's reign. What's more, archaeologists have found evidence of continued Buddhist building activity during Pushyamitra's reign, suggesting that the situation may have been more complex than the accounts describe. Still, the presence of such stories reveals that Pushyamitra's rule left strong impressions.

One fact is certain. Pushyamitra succeeded in bringing Magadha back to its feet. He strengthened tax collection in the core territories, reorganized local councils, and appointed officials who would not challenge his authority. Roads were also repaired, reviving trade activities, and borders were fortified.

Pushyamitra wore the crown for approximately thirty-six years, eventually establishing a dynasty known as the Shunga. He was then succeeded by Agnimitra in 149 BCE. As the son of Pushyamitra, Agnimitra was a capable ruler. He had served the empire earlier as governor, so he was well versed in the matters of the court by the time of his coronation. Agnimitra reigned for only eight years, but his contributions were impressive. Besides patronizing arts and literature, he is remembered for waging a successful war against the neighboring independent kingdom of Vidarbha. It's safe to assume that Agnimitra continued some of his father's policies while giving more attention to palace affairs and regional negotiations.

Unfortunately, after Agnimitra, the line of Shunga rulers grew weaker. Regional clans again grew bold to push for autonomy. There were signs of division among the court officials, and Pataliputra's nobles also began to prioritize their own positions over the stability of the empire. By the time Devabhuti inherited the throne in 83 BCE, the empire had once again lost much of the strength that Pushyamitra had built.

Devabhuti wasn't just the last king of his line. Many traditions describe him as inattentive to affairs of state. Some accounts record how he was easily distracted by court entertainment and found joy in the comforts of the palace. In other words, he was a ruler who preferred private pleasures to public responsibilities. Whether these descriptions were exaggerated by later writers or reflected his true nature remains uncertain, but the effect on the court is clear. When a king withdrew from his duties, others stepped forward to fill the space he left behind.

One person who took advantage of this was Vasudeva Kanva. As a senior minister, he held high influence in the court. He had already built connections among powerful nobles and aligned himself with those who believed the emperor had no desire to lead the empire. Vasudeva Kanva also oversaw messages that came in and out of the palace, managed the royal coffers, and had eyes on the movement of officials at all times. Unlike Devabhuti, Vasudeva paid close attention to the state's governance. Over time, many courtiers began to consult him rather than the ruler they were supposed to serve.

Ironically, the Shunga line ended in treachery—just like the Mauryan dynasty. According to Bāṇabhaṭṭa, a Sanskrit poet who lived many centuries later, Devabhuti was assassinated by Vasudeva Kanva, with the help of the daughter of a slave woman serving the emperor.

With the death of Devabhuti, Vasudeva Kanva made himself the new emperor of Magadha, establishing the Kanva dynasty. The Kanva rulers sat on the throne of Magadha from 73 BCE to 28 BCE. The Kanva's fall into the hands of the Satavahana dynasty marked the end of Magadha as a single, centralized power.

Chapter 6 – Women in Ancient India

One of the most popular epics of ancient India, the *Mahābhārata*, contains the story of a certain woman known by the name Draupadī. She is, in fact, one of the central characters of the ancient Sanskrit epic. Considered one of the most prominent figures in both Hindu and Indian culture, Draupadī is often noted for her beauty, courage, devotion, intelligence, resilience, and rhetorical skills. Even to this day, her story has been an inspiration for artists and performers alike.

According to the epic, Draupadī was a princess of the Panchala kingdom and the wife of the five royal Pāṇḍavas brothers named Yudhishthira, Bhima,

An illustration of Draupadī and the Pāṇḍavas brothers.[15]

Arjuna, Nakula, and Sahadeva. Their story, however, is not a romantic one, as it centers on a political disaster. The brothers were in a constant rivalry with their cousins, the Kauravas, who were described as deceitful.

One of the most famous episodes in the epic occurs when Yudhishthira, the eldest of the Pāṇḍava brothers, accepts a dice game proposed by the power-hungry Kauravas. Unaware that the game is rigged, he eventually gambles away everything he ever possessed. At first it's his wealth, then his kingdom, and finally, himself. Then, Draupadī enters the episode. She is dragged into the Sabha, the royal assembly hall, as part of the final wager. However, instead of responding with fear or submission, Draupadī remains composed. She asks nothing but a simple question:

"If my husband lost himself first, what legal rights does he have left to stake me?"

The Sabha is filled with powerful figures like Bhīṣma, the kingdom's senior statesman and authority on morality, Droṇa, the military commander, and Dhṛtarāṣṭra, the blind king presiding over the dispute. But none can answer her.

Her question breaks the court's moral paralysis. After a moment of prolonged silence, the blind king, Dhṛtarāṣṭra, responds. He grants her request for first Yudhishthira's freedom, then the freedom of the other Pāṇḍavas.

Of course, this story is literary, not historical. But it has shaped Indian cultural memory for centuries because it presents a woman who understands the mechanics of power better than the men around her.

Another major Indian epic, the *Rāmāyaṇa*, speaks of another female figure: Sītā, the wife of Rāma, a prince celebrated for his moral integrity and destined to be king. The story begins when Sītā is abducted by the ruler of Lanka, Rāvaṇa. With the support of his allies, Rāma eventually rescues her, but another conflict rises upon her return. Many doubt her purity. (This is a reflection of patriarchal expectations deeply embedded in the social values of the period. Often, a woman's honor was judged through standards imposed by the community rather than by her actions or intentions.)

An illustration of Sītā and her husband, Rāma.[16]

However, Sītā does not waste her time defending herself verbally. She knows that the only way to silence those who judge her is to show evidence. So, she chooses a response that defines her character for thousands of years: Sītā chooses to go through a test known as the *agniparikṣā*. In this trial by fire, Sītā steps into a burning pyre. There are many versions of the outcome, but the most popular one says that the fire deity, Agni, protects her. She emerges from the fire unharmed, proving her innocence. She is accepted back by Rāma and the court. The episode marks one of the most debated moments in the epic, reflecting the heavy moral expectations that women were often forced to shoulder.

Still, these two episodes illustrate something important about ancient Indian storytelling. Women are not merely background decorations. They serve as catalysts, challengers, and anchors for the moral and political dilemmas that drive both epics forward. Their actions are decisive, and the narrative revolves around their choices.

Needless to say, the historical reality of women in ancient India was complex. Their position was neither uniform nor static. Their status changed considerably across time, region, and social class, creating a landscape where empowerment and restriction often coexisted.

In the Early Vedic period (c. 1500–1000 BCE), textual evidence points to a society in which women were held in high regard. Not only were women of this period viewed as respected members of the household, but they were allowed to enjoy a degree of freedom that later eras refused to preserve. Young girls were given formal education, sometimes studying the same sacred texts as boys. Women were also given opportunities to participate in public rituals and philosophical discussions. In some cases, they composed hymns that made their way into the Vedic corpus.

Notable figures such as Gargī Vācaknavī, who debated metaphysics in the *Bṛhadāraṇyaka Upaniṣad,* and Maitreyī, who questioned the nature of immortality, appear in early texts as respected intellectuals.

Marriage also operated differently during this time. Women could choose their partners in certain contexts, and texts record forms of marriage where mutual consent was essential.

Religious life further reinforced this early pattern of respect. The worship of goddesses such as Sarasvatī (learning), Lakṣmī (prosperity), and Durgā (strength and protection) was already well established. These were far from being minor deities. In fact, these goddesses were considered central figures in ritual life, reflecting a worldview in which feminine power—*Śakti*—was seen as fundamental to cosmic order.

But as time passed, this landscape gradually changed. In the later Vedic and post-Vedic periods, women became subject to more rigid patriarchal norms. Legal and didactic texts from these eras began to define women primarily through their roles as daughters, wives, and mothers. The flexibility of earlier centuries gave way to greater emphasis on male authority and female obedience. Sadly, the freedoms and rights women once enjoyed became increasingly limited to specific communities or elite groups.

This change can also be seen in social practices that gained prominence in later periods. Child marriage became more common, narrowing the span of a woman's autonomy. The dowry system, though not uniform across the subcontinent, placed additional economic burdens on families with daughters. This also led to the perception of women as financial liabilities. In theory, property rights existed, particularly the concept of *strīdhan,* property gifted to a woman at marriage. But widows often lost inheritance claims, and remarriage was never a good option since it could strip them of earlier rights.

Despite these tightening restrictions, women did not disappear from political or administrative life. In certain dynasties and regional polities, women still exercised genuine authority. The kingdom of Magadha, for instance, felt the influence of powerful female figures such as Queen Nandini. She was often associated with diplomacy, intrigue, and political maneuvering during the era of the Nanda dynasty. Elsewhere, inscriptions and narratives mention queens managing estates, issuing land grants, or ruling as regents when political circumstances demanded it. These examples do not negate the broader decline in women's freedoms, but they show that female leadership was not entirely removed from the historical record.

The Controversial Story of Tishyarakshita

This story takes place during the reign of Ashoka. The emperor was said to have multiple queens who gave birth to several sons. Of course, each of these sons were backed by different circles of influence with their own interests. Ministers, attendants, and relatives all held different opinions on who should wear the crown next. It was during this period of tension that Tishyarakshita appears in the literary record.

An illustration of Tishyarakshita.[17]

Tishyarakshita's name did not come from administrative archives or inscriptions. Instead, her image comes almost entirely from Buddhist narrative texts such as the *Ashokavadana* and *Divyāvadāna*, both of which were written centuries after Ashoka's life. These sources are valuable, but they were also shaped by moral lessons, sectarian interests, and narrative convention. This means they must be approached with caution.

In these accounts, Tishyarakshita is introduced as a younger wife of Ashoka. She is described as intelligent, perceptive, and very involved in courtly matters. However, the Buddhist authors place her firmly in the role of an antagonistic queen, following a pattern seen in many South Asian literary traditions in which powerful royal women are depicted as jealous or dangerous to highlight a moral point. Her story centers on one of Ashoka's sons, Kunala. According to the Buddhist legends, he was exceptionally handsome, virtuous, and devoted to the principles of dhamma.

According to most Buddhist authors, this episode took place when Kunala visited a distant province to serve as the governor on behalf of Ashoka. Before he set out for this journey, he was stopped by Tishyarakshita. Some speak of their meeting in the palace, others during a ceremonial gathering. Whichever the venue, Tishyarakshita was believed to have developed an infatuation the moment she laid eyes on the prince. Kunala, however, rejected her advances, reminding her that she was his own stepmother.

Tishyarakshita was enraged by the rejection, though she did not exact revenge immediately. One day, while Ashoka was deeply asleep, she quietly took a letter the emperor had prepared to be sent to the ministers in Taxila, where Kunala was stationed. She altered the message, changing a word in the Prakrit script from *adheetaam* ("he must study") to *andheetaam* ("he must be blinded"). Tishyarakshita then sealed the letter carefully, making it appear as if it was untouched.

When the letter arrived in Taxila, the ministers were horrified. They showed signs of hesitation until Kunala strongly advised them to do as the emperor wished. According to another version, Kunala himself read the order and blinded himself with a hot iron as an act of obedience. Regardless, Tishyarakshita succeeded in her plan.

Kunala and his wife, Kanchanmala were left with no choice but to wander the land as beggars, surviving only by playing music. Ashoka eventually discovered what happened to his son. Overwhelmed by grief and enraged at his wife's treachery, the Mauryan emperor punished Tishyarakshita severely: she was executed.

But, as we said, this event is not corroborated by historical evidence. The complete silence on this in Ashoka's inscriptions suggests that the dramatic story preserved in Buddhist literature belongs to a later interpretive tradition. The Buddhist writers use this moment to reinforce the king's commitment to justice and the karmic consequences of unethical behavior.

There are also political explanations that fit the situation more plausibly. Ashoka had several sons, and Kunala was not the clear successor. His mother, according to some traditions, was not a principal queen, which may have weakened his position. A queen advocating for her own son's claim was not unusual. Neither was political maneuvering to diminish the influence of rival branches of the royal family. In this light, the story of Tishyarakshita's romantic jealousy could be a later embellishment imposed on what was originally a succession struggle. The Buddhist chroniclers, viewing the court from a moral lens, might have reframed political conflict as a tale of personal misconduct.

Still, the persistence of her story, however hostile the sources, implies that she was not a marginal figure. Even if the details are distorted, her presence in these legends indicates that she was remembered, however imperfectly, as someone whose actions influenced debates over succession and legitimacy. That alone places her among the women whose imprint on ancient Indian political life survived the centuries, even if only through the lens of those who disapproved of her.

Ambapālī, One of the Most Influential Women of Ancient Vaiśālī

Before the Mauryan Empire came to dominate northern India, the city of Vaiśālī was best known for its unique politics. Unlike most of the cities on the subcontinent, Vaiśālī was not ruled by a single monarch. Instead, it operated as a republic governed by an assembly of clan leaders known as the Licchavis. Under this system, certain public roles carried both prestige and responsibility. Among them was the position of *nagarvadhu*, a term that translates to either "bride of the city" or "the city courtesan."

Far from being marginalized, the *nagarvadhu* was an officially recognized figure representing refinement, culture, and artistic accomplishment. The title was reserved only for highly talented and beautiful courtesans in ancient India. They often performed at public events, acted as a patron of the arts, and of course, were expected to interact with the social and political elite.

Our main character, Ambapālī, belonged to this class. Her reputation was preserved in Buddhist texts and local traditions, which often described her as graceful, talented, and highly sought after by both nobles and visiting dignitaries. Her origins, however, vary depending on the source. According to one popular legend, she was discovered as an infant under a mango tree. This gave her the name Ambapālī, which simply meant "the mango-grove girl." This origin story is typical of literary traditions that seek to elevate a figure by giving them an unusual beginning.

An ivory carving depicting Ambapālī (right) greeting Buddha.[18]

A more grounded explanation suggests she was trained and appointed as the city courtesan because of her unparalleled skills. In a republic like Vaiśālī, where cultural events played a diplomatic role, the *nagarvadhu* needed to be not only educated but also musically accomplished and socially adept—and Ambapālī excelled in all these qualities.

One of the clearest signs of Ambapālī's standing was her ownership of her own estate, which included a well-known mango grove. This was unusual, especially when not all women were given the same property rights. Often, their rights depended on context and caste. According to traditional narratives, her estate was valuable enough that the Licchavi nobles sought to acquire it for themselves. Records preserved in Buddhist texts describe how they attempted to pressure her into relinquishing it by using their political authority to challenge her ownership.

But Ambapālī was always firm; she would not easily yield. She resisted the nobles' pressure by continuously asserting her legal rights and leveraging her public position. In the end, she retained her property. The dispute reveals how firmly she stood within Vaiśālī's political and social framework. Clearly, she was not merely an entertainer completely dependent on patrons. She was a figure with her own autonomy, wealth, and legal standing in one of the most powerful republics of the time.

Her interactions with nobility were not limited to local politics. Later, merchants and even kings sought her company not solely for pleasure but because an association with the *nagarvadhu* of Vaiśālī was a mark of prestige. This gave her a form of unwritten influence. People in high positions treated her with the same seriousness they reserved for political allies.

Ambapālī's later life is most clearly preserved through the *Therīgāthā*, an ancient anthology of poems composed by early Buddhist nuns. A set of verses attributed to her offers a rare first-person reflection on aging and the passage of time. These verses describe the fading of her youthful beauty without sentimentality. She lists specific parts of her body (hair, skin, limbs) and notes how they have changed. However, she frames her transformation as an inevitable process rather than a source of sorrow. The tone is introspective, matter of fact, and grounded in the Buddhist emphasis on impermanence.

These verses are also remarkable because they represent one of the earliest forms of women's autobiographical writing in India. Through them, Ambapālī speaks with her own voice, not filtered through the perspectives of male authors. They offer an unembellished glimpse into her self-understanding as a woman who once occupied a position of public admiration and later embraced a life of renunciation.

Bhadda Kundalakesa, the Woman Who Debated Anyone

Bhadda Kundalakesa was born into a wealthy merchant family. The beginning of her story, however, is intertwined with a certain boy. Unlike Bhadda, the boy's birth was accompanied with ominous signs—though the records never mention exact details. His parents, worried that he might bring misfortune, initially considered putting him to death. But they eventually had a change of heart and raised him.

Those signs later proved accurate. As he grew older, the boy developed a compulsive habit of stealing. He would take whatever he could reach without regard for consequences. His parents did everything to set him right. They scolded and punished him, but he continued stealing. When he reached adulthood and showed no ability beyond this compulsion, his father gave him the means to become a professional thief and left him to his own fate.

What followed was predictable. The young man broke into so many houses that news of his crimes reached the royal court. Enraged, the king gave his officers a single day to find the culprit or face execution themselves. Under such pressure, the thief was caught quickly and sentenced to death.

This is the moment Bhadda enters the story. As the thief was led through the city on the way to his punishment, Bhadda saw him. For reasons unknown, love manifested. Bhadda felt an intense attachment to him and immediately begged her father to interfere and secure his release. After being persuaded, the king granted a pardon, and the thief was made Bhadda's husband.

Unfortunately, even after coming close to death itself, the thief remained unchanged. He continued to steal, and soon, his target was none other than the person who had saved his life. He noticed that Bhadda always wore expensive ornaments, so he devised a plan to kill her and escape with her jewelry. He lured her to a remote spot at the edge of a cliff. His plan was to push her off the cliff and remove her ornaments. But Bhadda was quick to discover his schemes. And so, she acted first and killed him.

Returning to her family after killing her husband, despite it being self-defense, was not an option. Concerned with social fallout and the uncertainty of her position, Bhadda made a drastic decision. She renounced the world and joined a Jain ascetic order. (The stories note that Jain nuns had their own hermitages and traveled widely, suggesting that female renunciants were a recognized and visible presence in ancient India.) Bhadda entered their ranks, setting her on the path that would define her reputation for the rest of her life.

Once she embraced the ascetic life, Bhadda's sharp intelligence quickly became her defining trait. Wandering ascetics across different traditions frequently engaged in public debates, which were typically held in marketplaces, courtyards, or public parks. These debates drew large audiences and often shaped a sect's reputation.

Bhadda excelled in this environment, and her reputation grew tremendously. Early sources depict her as articulate and quick-thinking. She was adept at exposing weaknesses in opposing arguments. Bhadda would travel from town to town, challenging philosophers, priests, and other renunciants. Legends claim that she rarely lost.

Although embellished by tradition, these stories suggest an important historical core: Bhadda built a reputation not through noble birth or political marriage but through impressive intellectual prowess. She operated comfortably in a domain normally dominated by men, and she earned respect—as well as notoriety—on her own terms.

Her most prominent stage of life was when she crossed paths with Sāriputta. As expected, Bhadda invited him to a debate. She was confident that her reasoning could withstand any opponent, even one of the Buddha's foremost disciples. She threw question after question to Sāriputta, but he answered each one smoothly. When she finally lost the debate, Bhadda did not have a fit. Instead, she learned the limitations of her training. According to Buddhist texts, she realized that she had mastered argumentation, but argument alone could not provide the insight she sought. Impressed by Sāriputta's responses in the debate, she requested ordination in the Buddhist order.

Bhadda Kundalakesa's story, like many preserved in Buddhist literature, blends historical memory with a pinch or two of legend. The basic elements, including her marriage, the cliffside incident, her time with the Jainas, her debating career, and her eventual conversion, likely reflect real traditions about a well-known female ascetic. The dramatic framing of her defeat by Sāriputta, however, bears the imprint of didactic storytelling.

Even so, her presence across multiple sources and her own surviving verses show that she was remembered as a striking figure. To this day, she is viewed as an example of a woman of intellect, self-determination, and formidable presence in the debates that animated ancient India's religious landscape.

Chapter 7 – The Arrival of the Horsemen: A Reimagination

The Byzantines knew them as the Hephthalites. Others referred to them as White Huns. Indian sources, however, call them the Hunas. These people came all the way from a realm that stretched across the lands north of the Hindu Kush, touching regions known today as Kazakhstan, Uzbekistan, and the western edges of Xinjiang. They were also different from the Huns who troubled the Roman Empire.

These regions were challenging, shaped by harsh winters and open steppe. It was nearly impossible for the Hunas to stay in one place permanently. When supplies dwindled and mother nature turned into a challenge, they must search and move to another location, building everything from scratch once more. These people soon moved into India, wreaking havoc across the flourishing Gupta Empire.

It's safe to say that the Hunas were one of the fiercest groups of horsemen to ever exist in Central Asia. Their children were expected to learn to stay balanced on a galloping horse before they could even speak clearly. Apart from being skillful at maneuvering a lightning-fast steed, the Hunas were also described to be exceptional in mounted archery. These were some of the skills that allowed them to push into Bactria, contest with the other steppe groups, and even test the strength of the Persian kings. Victory was not always theirs, but they could always learn a lesson from each encounter.

Of course, raiding was not one of their hobbies. Nomadic tribes typically embarked on migrations or invasions when the plains they called home were growing crowded, exhausted, or threatened by new rising clans.

And so, when the Hunas heard word of a wealthy and fertile land that lay to the south beyond the jagged barrier of the Hindu Kush, they were quick to strategize their surprise arrival. The Gupta Empire appeared mighty to the untrained eye, but it was beginning to rot from within—and the Hunas knew this. An empire might be strong, but none were impregnable forever.

The riders mounted their horses and began their long descent to the south in the mid fifth century CE. At this time, their name was still unknown in the lands they approached. But it wouldn't take long for that to change.

The State of the Gupta Empire

The Gupta Empire is considered India's classical golden age. It rose to prominence sometime in 320 CE under Chandragupta I and reached its zenith under his successors, Samudragupta and Chandragupta II. With its location lying across the Gangetic Plain, the dynasty was bestowed with luxurious gifts: fertile fields, busy trade routes, and old urban centers—all of which contributed to its massive wealth and authority.

The Gupta Empire was known for stability and refined administration. Under the reign of the Gupta rulers, cities like Pataliputra, Ujjain, and Mathura bloomed like never before. They transformed into important centers of learning, commerce, and religious activity.

Gupta rulers prioritized art, literature, and knowledge. They frequently supported poets, scholars, and artisans whose works shaped the memory of early Indian civilization. This period marked the flourishing of Sanskrit literature and the expansion of knowledge in astronomy and mathematics.

Sculptors and metalworkers also produced some of their best creations during this time. The seated Buddha from Sarnath (near Varanasi), for instance, is a prime example of the Gupta period's artistic style, which fascinates art historians to this day. Later images of the Buddha in India and Southeast Asia were heavily influenced by this very style.

Trade with lands to the west and across the Indian Ocean also kept markets active and ports bustling with color. To many within the core of the empire, it seemed like a period of confidence and cultural richness, a time when the world felt orderly and the boundaries of the kingdom secure. It was easy to fall into the illusion of security. Many believed that the empire's trouble ended at the borders and could never trespass into its great halls.

But the more influence and fame an empire secured, the bigger the threat it would soon face.

Rumor on the Frontier

It was just after sunrise that the man guarding the watchtower at the edge of Gandhara noticed approaching visitors. This frontier post was located far from the comforts of the big cities, so a single glance across the horizon could easily alert the guards.

However, this time, the guests were not enemies. It was a caravan that seemed more anxious than usual. The traders had dust on their clothing, and their animals looked tired, as if they had been pushing harder than usual. Suddenly, one of the merchants stepped forward, greeting the guards in a slow voice. He did not bring the usual chatter about markets, roads, or precious goods they had just traded. Instead, he brought a rumor-something that had shaken his men enough that they spoke of it only once they were inside the safety of the outpost walls.

The merchant claimed that, beyond the passes, a village had been burned to the ground. The attack must have been swift, he said, too fast for villagers to mount a defense. The raiders moved in and vanished before anyone could identify who they were. He also informed the guards about their strange discovery in the ashes: small metal pieces marked with unfamiliar patterns. They certainly did not belong to the Guptas or the Kushan. They were also not older coins from the northwest.

Then, another merchant added more detail to the news. He had heard rumors that these riders were not like the settled clans of the region. Instead, they rode smaller, tougher horses and were armed with bows that could bend farther than Indian archers believed possible.

The officer in charge of the outpost listened without interrupting. The news was not exactly surprising to him since he had heard vague hints of such riders in recent seasons. But this was the first time anyone had traveled directly from a burned settlement. Quickly, he ordered the guards to record the information shared by the weary traders and sent a messenger east with a report.

The Beginning of an End

There was no sign of unease in the east. Life in the capital at Pataliputra resumed as usual. The morning opened with the sound of conch shells, temple bells, and the low voices of scholars politely greeting one another in the shaded courtyards. The sky was clear, as if it was just another beautiful, uninterrupted day. The sunlight shone against the gilded ornaments atop palace roofs, making the city appear majestic, especially to newcomers.

Market stalls were already open along the main streets. They each displayed their best goods, ranging from spices to carved ivory, fine textiles, and metalwork that never failed to draw merchants from across the region. When caravans arrived from the ports of the west, they brought goods from Persia and lands farther still. Meanwhile, from the eastern roads came traders from Bengal, their boats often laden with cloth and grains.

The atmosphere inside the palace complex was even more vibrant. Courtiers could be seen making their way toward the audience chamber, while scribes were busy carrying bundles of palm leaf manuscripts to a meeting. There were artists who brought their pigments and boards, ready for another day's work in service of the court. Meanwhile, in a shaded alcove, a group of Brahmins were debating a philosophical question. A pair of Buddhist monks stood at another corner, discussing a line from a recent sermon.

Elsewhere in the palace, a poet recited a few new verses to a small audience of nobles. Among them was a man whose reputation was beginning to rise beyond the court. Known as Kalidasa, he would go down in history as the greatest Sanskrit poet and dramatist of all time. He listened to the young poet with a half smile, occasionally offering a suggestion to refine a line or strengthen an image.

In a hall where land grants were being issued, several officials could be seen gathering for a meeting. Brahmins and administrators had their days full of reviewing documents and recording the rights given to temples, scholars, and loyal officers.

At the edge of this hall, a lone messenger stood, freshly arrived from the frontier. In his hands was a report sealed with the mark of an outpost in Gandhara. He gently placed the scroll among the other documents, but unsurprisingly, none of the officials reached for it right away. After all, Pataliputra favored good news far more than warning. The officials were so absorbed in their discussions about lands and festivals for the coming season that they were certain that whatever news had come from the northwest could wait until the morning's work was done.

But the messenger waited, shifting his weight slowly from one foot to another. He watched as scribes moved past him without a glance. For a moment, he wondered if the court had grown too accustomed to peace, too certain of its own strength. But he said nothing. He had delivered his report, and its fate was no longer in his hands.

Fortunately, the warning did not fall entirely on deaf ears. Word of the disturbances soon reached a man who deeply understood the weight of such news better than most. A prince named Skandagupta, he was renowned for his discipline and resolve. He had grown up hearing stories of his forefathers' campaigns—tales of Samudragupta's sweeping victories and Chandragupta's steady rule. So, as the son of the Gupta emperor Kumaragupta I, he knew that it was his responsibility to protect the legacy he had inherited.

However, he received the report of the disturbances not from reading the scroll dropped by the messenger in Pataliputra but while overseeing military inspections in the western provinces. He knew that trouble was brewing. More reports came in later. The outpost at Gandhara had fallen mysteriously silent, a minor chief had shown signs of shifting his loyalty, and a merchant relay station had been destroyed. These confirmed his suspicions that something new had arrived at the fringes of the empire.

Without delay, Skandagupta summoned his council of generals. They gathered inside a fort that overlooked a dry valley. The meeting, however, opened with confusion rather than clarity. Some officers insisted that the enemy must be remnants of old regional clans they had previously defeated that were growing bolder once more. Others pointed to rebellious groups from beyond the Indus. But the descriptions brought by traders did not match any known enemy.

"If these rumors have truth to them, then it is best we make a move," one of the generals may have said.

Skandagupta agreed and immediately issued orders. He sent scouts and armies to the west. There was undoubtedly no room for caution. Skandagupta himself refused to remain behind the walls as his men set out. He marched at the head of a mixed force: infantry seasoned by earlier campaigns, cavalry units drawn from loyal chiefs, and a few elephant corps positioned to anchor the line.

Their first confrontation took place at dusk. It began with the return of Skandagupta's scouts, who warned the rest that the hostile riders were approaching. It is said that the prince barely had time to reposition his lines when the enemy swept down the slope, their steeds kicking up clouds of dust. They rode with astonishing speed. Their movements were fluid and scattered at the same time. Instead of forming a solid front, they broke into smaller groups, circling the Gupta ranks. Then, they released a rain of arrows from bows that bent far more than those used by Indian archers.

The attack took Skandagupta's forces by surprise. It scattered the units at first, but the prince quickly steadied them. He led the infantry forward and called the cavalry to flank the enemy. Then, the elephant corps made their move, leaving the riders no choice but to retreat from close engagement. After a tense and chaotic struggle, the raiders finally withdrew. Swiftly, they disappeared into the horizon. Skandagupta's men erupted in celebration as they watched their enemies retreat, but the prince remained quiet.

Bodies lay across the field, Gupta soldiers among them. Their armor was pierced by arrows that were lighter, sharper, and built for speed. Skandagupta took his time surveying the ground. He was now certain that these riders were not a familiar enemy simply testing the border. The battlefield belonged to him that day, but this skirmish was just the beginning of their problem—or perhaps, their collapse.

Not long after that first clash, the signs of strain reached the city of Mathura. The merchants in its sprawling bazaar had always been early risers, pulling open wooden shutters at dawn and calling for their apprentices to arrange their goods. But now their voices carried less confidence. News traveled along the trade roads fast, sometimes faster than caravans. By the time the first travelers from the northwest limped into Mathura, their stories were already being spread around.

A cloth merchant who had once greeted customers with a loud, cheerful call would now pause his activities whenever he heard hoofbeats echoing through the streets. He had heard from a passing caravan that a small market town to the north had been raided—not conquered or held, only struck, plundered, and left in the smoke. Nobody knew which settlement would be next. From that point on, the merchant found himself scanning the roads more often than the faces of buyers who browsed his stall.

Along the riverbanks, monks who had lived peacefully in small monasteries outside the city gates began arriving in groups. They carried little more than the robes on their backs and a few scrolls they refused to abandon. Their monasteries, they said, were too exposed. Too far from the safety of walls. They sought refuge in Mathura's larger temples, where they hoped the sound of chanting and the presence of travelers might offer some protection. Artisans followed the same path. Metalworkers and potters grew wary of the safety of their families, so they packed up their workshops and moved toward the crowded quarters near the main market.

Prices changed quickly. Grains cost more with each passing week. Caravans from the northwest arrived late or did not arrive at all. Spices that had once come regularly from mountain towns became rare. When they appeared, they were often sold for double the usual rate. Some merchants also spoke of coins marked with strange symbols carried by traders fleeing the frontier. Nobody recognized them at first, but eventually someone named the riders who minted them: the Huna.

The pressure was felt by everyone, even the city's chiefs. Their most important duty had long been to protect Mathura and keep its gates secure. However, now their decisions were tangled in doubt. Some urged loyalty to the Gupta throne in Pataliputra, insisting that reinforcements would soon arrive. Others believed that waiting for distant help was foolish. If the Huna reached Mathura, they argued, it would be safer for the city to negotiate its own survival. Quietly, a few chiefs began making their own preparations regardless of what the emperor decreed.

As Mathura braced itself for impending threats, another change was taking shape far to the east. Sometime in 450 CE, Emperor Kumaragupta I had died. He had worn the crown for slightly over a decade, and his early reign was often remembered as a period of stability and prosperity. His influence could be felt across the vast land, from Gujarat in the west to Bengal in the east. The emperor was also credited with founding the famous Nalanda University in Bihar. But as he stepped closer to the end of his life, uncertainty grew. Apart from the riders, the empire itself was also battling internal issues: governors in distant regions had become more independent.

So, the transition that followed Kumaragupta's passing was not as smooth as earlier successions. Court factions argued day and night, each shouting support to different claimants. For a moment, it was unclear who would take the throne and lead the empire back to its feet.

Inscriptions from Skandagupta's later years speak of how he eventually worked his way to the throne, becoming a worthy successor. After removing the other claimants, he secured the loyalty of the army, which remembered the discipline and resolve he had shown during the first clash with the riders. It did not take long for the officials, especially those who valued stability, to line up behind him. They were convinced that only a firm hand at the center could keep the empire from slipping further into disorder.

Skandagupta was accepted as the next Gupta emperor, yet his work did not end with his coronation. Reports from the northwest continued to arrive, each more troubling than the last. The riders who had tested the border while he was still a prince were returning with greater strength. This time, they had successfully taken Gandhara and established a firmer foothold.

And so, the emperor prepared for another campaign. Some would say that this disturbance accelerated his age. The weight of command had carved lines on his face, and sleepless nights had become familiar companions. He knew that his first clash with the Hunas years earlier was just a warning. This time, the riders had come prepared and were determined to push deeper into Gupta territory.

However, Skandagupta was never known to back down easily. He gathered what remained of his strongest units and advanced again to the northwest. The journey itself tested the men. Supplies were thinner, horses needed rest more often, and the treasury that once supported large armies had been depleted due to the succession struggle following the death of Kumaragupta I. It was a struggle to fund even a single campaign. Still, they moved on, driven by the knowledge that the frontier would not hold without them.

The next battle erupted somewhere near the Punjab region, where open fields coincided with rocky ground. The Huna riders struck at them with the same precision Skandagupta and his men remembered. Volleys of arrows filled the sky, and the riders circled the Guptas in sweeping arcs. Then, they vanished, leaving only clouds of dust, before reappearing again in sudden bursts. The Gupta infantry stood their ground. They raised their shields and waited for the perfect moment to counterattack.

It was a brutal struggle. Skandagupta fought in the center, rallying his men as lines bent under the force of the heavy charges. Hours passed before the tide finally turned. In the end, the Hunas retreated and made their way north, leaving behind their fallen.

Skandagupta had emerged victorious again, but it tasted strangely hollow. The battlefield was covered with bodies. Many were his own soldiers, men who would not return to their villages or families. Worse still was the cost that awaited him in the capital. The empire's treasury was nearly empty. To rebuild the army for the next threat, taxes would have to increase. Farmers would be the ones to suffer, as they had to pay more. Merchants, too, would not be excluded. Everyone would feel the burden of keeping the invaders away.

The brave emperor understood a truth that few dared to speak aloud. This latest victory was only temporary. He was merely holding back collapse, not restoring the empire that his ancestors had tirelessly built. Each campaign drained more strength than it returned. Even as the court celebrated his latest success, he knew that the future was slipping beyond his grasp. There was little he could do to permanently keep the Guptas from harm.

There are no exact details of his death, but historians agree that Skandagupta likely ruled until 468 CE. His death plunged the empire into a time of turmoil. Some say he left behind no heir to claim the throne, so it was passed to his half-brother, Purugupta. The Gupta dynasty remained in control for many more years, but none of the rulers that came after Skandagupta could reverse the damage the empire was suffering.

Internal issues continued to swell. Across the provinces, governors began acting as if they were kings in their own right. They collected taxes for themselves, not always for the court. They negotiated with border tribes without waiting for permission from Pataliputra. Some even raised personal armies. The unity that once defined the Mauryas and the early Guptas had clearly disappeared. Trade routes that had once carried merchants from city to city now felt unsafe. Caravans traveled in smaller groups, avoiding certain roads entirely. Farmers who once relied on stability to plant their crops found themselves subjected to new taxes imposed by whatever official claimed the land that year.

Half a century after Skandagupta's victory against the invaders, the Hunas returned to the borders once more. This time, they were led by a formidable warrior named Toramana. Under his command, the riders pushed deep into northern India, this time achieving major success. Towns fell, leaving behind only smoke and ashes. Local chiefs who valued their lives more than loyalty to Pataliputra either surrendered to the invaders or offered a hand to help them push deeper into the empire. For a time, Toramana held sway over regions of central India, carving his authority into the land with surprising speed.

Then, around 515 CE, the torch of leadership was passed to his son, Mihirakula. This name was remembered especially by Buddhist chroniclers, who cited him as a harsh ruler. They described how he never thought twice about destroying monasteries as long as his invasion missions could make progress. Monks began to flee south the moment they heard rumors that the riders were closing in. Of course, these accounts tend to be exaggerated.

Other sources painted a more mixed picture. Some regions acknowledged Mihirakula as a legitimate king. Even his court soon displayed elements of Indian courtly culture. His coins carried symbols familiar to the people he ruled, and his use of elephants in battle suggested a growing acceptance of local military traditions.

By this time, the Guptas were already severely weakened and divided. With their economic strain and internal power struggles, it was impossible for them to push the Hunas back permanently. Historians suggest that environmental stress and potential climatic disasters further contributed to the empire's decline. Gradually, the Guptas authority shrank to small regions, then to single cities. In the end, the empire that had once produced the best poets, mathematicians, sculptors, and astronomers of all time dissolved into a constellation of smaller kingdoms.

Yet the Huna riders were never destined to rule the land forever. Resistance grew as regional rulers gathered strength. In the sixth century CE, coalitions of Indian kings made a move, slowly pushing back the invaders. In central India, leaders such as Yashodharman of Malwa successfully launched attacks that corroded Huna authority. Bit by bit, their strongholds were breached and broken. As a result, some Huna groups retreated toward the northwest, while others settled more quietly, blending into local communities.

With the Gupta empire now a thing of the past, India entered a new and more fragmented age. Smaller kingdoms rose in the regions once controlled by the Guptas. In the north, particularly in places like Magadha and Kanauj, new dynasties were born, each competing for complete influence. Meanwhile, in the west, rulers at Valabhi prioritized trade activities. They were the ones who guarded the trade routes and coastal ports. Farther east, different courts began to shape their own versions of kingship and culture. Although no single power replaced the Guptas at once, many of these later states inherited their systems of administration, their styles of art, and even their memory of what a strong and orderly kingdom should look like.

Chapter 8 – What Life Was Really Like in the Gupta Empire

An Astronomer in Ujjain

Dawn had just made its first appearance of the day, shining its cool early light on the rooftops of Ujjain, the beating heart of arts and literature in the Gupta Empire. The Shipra River, a sacred river comparable to the Ganga River, still held the night's last chill. A few early risers walked down the *ghāṭ* (a flight of steps typically found by the riverbank) to perform their ablutions.

The Shipra River today.[19]

Meanwhile, on the city's northern hill stood a cluster of buildings belonging to a small school of astronomers. This was the place where calculations were made long before the day's bustle reached the markets, where scholars measured the heavens with the same seriousness kings devoted to politics. This was where our astronomer, Rishyashva, spent most of his time. He had been awake before the first light breached through the skies. Like many others in his discipline, he preferred the quiet hours when the mind felt unburdened.

Sitting cross-legged on a reed mat, Rishyashva was surrounded by palm-leaf manuscripts. He had a lot to go through today. So, he tied his cotton shawl more tightly around his shoulders and began reading through a manuscript containing a set of eclipse tables copied from an earlier *siddhānta* (textbook). It was another ordinary morning, but for an intellectual like him, no morning ever passed without a small thrill of responsibility.

A few hours later, a young apprentice arrived. He greeted Rishyashva with a small bow before inviting the middle-aged scholar outside. When Rishyashva stepped out into the courtyard, the eastern horizon had begun to shift from grey to pale gold. A few of his younger students were still rubbing their eyes as they prepared the instruments on the rooftop. One of the instruments was called a *śaṅku*. Planted upright on the polished stone floor, the *śaṅku* was a crucial tool to determine latitude, solstice drift, and midday shadows.

Rishyashva bent to examine the first shadow cast by the *śaṅku* while his apprentice marked its tip carefully with a charcoal dot. In time, they would compare the curve of these markings to yesterday's and the previous day's. Precision mattered. A single miscalculated angle could easily ruin a table of rising times, and a ruined table meant a flawed calendar, which in turn could disrupt temple festivals and ceremonial timing across the surrounding towns.

If the day was cloudy and no sunlight shone from the heavens, scholars would use another method to measure time. Known as the *ghaṭikā-yantra* (a water clock used to track time through controlled dripping), it was a simple device but remarkably reliable when handled with care. Used both in ancient times and the medieval era, this instrument featured a small thin metal bowl with a pin-sized hole at its base. The bowl was placed gently upon the surface of water inside a larger vessel.

Once set afloat, the bowl would begin to fill as water seeped in through the tiny hole. The rhythm of that seepage allowed scholars to mark the passage of fixed units of time. When the bowl finally sank, its descent signaled that one *ghaṭikā* had passed.

By mid-morning, Ujjain became even more lively. Women could be seen gathering at the *ghāṭ*, washing utensils and cloth. A few brought their children along to splash in the shallow waters. Merchants began to fill the marketplace, each hurriedly raising the shutters of his stalls, eager to start another day of business. On the other side of the city, priests walked briskly toward the temple with brass pots of water balanced on their hips.

Time seemed to never stop for Rishyashva as task after task arrived to fill his day. A messenger approached him, having traveled from a nearby shrine. He carried a clay tablet on which a question was etched in a rather hurried stroke. Rishyashva read it twice to fully absorb the inquiry. The priests wished to know the correct rising time of Jupiter for an upcoming consecration ceremony. Such requests were common, as many rituals depended on planetary positions.

Rishyashva walked over to a table where his manuscripts were neatly stacked. After scanning the latest position tables and comparing them with that morning's shadow measurements, he gave a faint smile. Jupiter was indeed cooperative this season. He dictated the calculations confidently to his apprentice, who wrote them on a fresh strip of palm leaf before dusting it with fine ash to dry the ink. The messenger took the document and thanked the scholars before hurrying off to deliver it to the priests.

Next, Rishyashva's routine brought him to another courtyard where students had already gathered. They were all seated under the neem tree with wooden writing boards ready in their laps. Although these young men were devoted learners of science and mathematics, they were no different from students anywhere else: the first row was attentive, the middle row hopeful, and the back row half-asleep.

Today's lesson revolved around *nakṣatras* (lunar mansions or constellations used to track the moon's monthly path). Rishyashva began the class by drawing a rough diagram and explaining how the moon's movement through the twenty-seven *nakṣatras* determined timing for certain rituals. He cited an older authority, then compared that authority with newer observations. Some students murmured agreement, while others frowned, struggling to reconcile theory with measurement. Rishyashva knew their struggle well. The heavens were consistent in their patterns, but human tools—be it rods, cords, or even human eyes—were far from perfect. Mistakes were bound to happen, but perhaps with knowledge, patience, repeated observation, and experience, they would not happen as often.

His lecture ended just before midday. This was the only time Rishyashva would sit and relax. He returned to the shaded veranda where a pot of buttermilk sat, cooling in a basin of water. The scholar drank slowly, appreciating what little free time he had that day. However, right after he took the first bite of his meal, a colleague arrived with a stack of palm leaves under his arm.

"A correction from Mathura," his colleague said, handing him the bundle. "Unfortunately, their calculation for the last eclipse does not match ours."

Rishyashva sighed. Harmonizing calculations across regions was perhaps the most tedious aspect of his work. Different academies used slightly different standards for the year's length, the moon's motion, and positional corrections. To say he was tired was an understatement, but he must see to the calculation. He made a mental note to review the discrepancy after lunch.

Ujjain's heat softened toward evening, and Rishyashva returned to the courtyard where the *śaṅku* stood once more for final observations. His apprentice, hardworking as ever, was already waiting for him, ready to jot down his observations. When the stars began to dot the dark sky, the two scholars would gather once more. This time, their station was on a platform built on the rooftop. Rishyashva would observe the position of the star while his apprentice recorded his reading meticulously.

Only after they finished the last of their measurements and readings did they descend the stairs, preparing themselves to end the day. By this time of day, Ujjain had grown quiet except for the sound of distant drums from a small shrine, marking the start of the evening ritual. There was nothing but oil lamps glowing in the doorways and other scholars calmly leaving the courtyard to return to their families. As for Rishyashva, he folded his palm-leaf manuscripts carefully before heading home, knowing that tomorrow he would return to the same chambers and courtyards once again, observing and calculating the universe.

The Guild Merchant from Uttarāpatha

Devendra jolted upright, startled by the sound of oxen shifting their yokes outside. He had spent the night in a rest house maintained by his guild—a low mud-brick structure located just off the main road east of Ujjain. Of course, comfort was minimal. The walls were bare and the floor hard. But at least there was a roof that kept Devendra from the dew and a doorway that faced a pleasing view of the Uttarāpatha—a major trade route bridging the city of Takshashila (modern Taxila) in the northwest to Tamralipti (modern Tamluk) on the Bay of Bengal in the east.

Immediately, Devendra reached for his ledger. This time, the bundle of goods was not large. But still, it was varied enough to matter. Some of these goods belonged to Devendra, while others were entrusted to him by fellow members of his *śreṇī* (merchant guild that organized trade and protected its members). There were rolls of fine cotton sitting in the corner, beautifully dyed with indigo and madder. Next to the cotton rolls were three chests. One was full of strings of glass beads, another had packets of black pepper, and the last carried several small copper vessels, each polished to a soft shine.

After checking each item, ensuring that none were stolen or broken, Devendra stepped out into the courtyards. He was not alone; a few other merchants were already preparing their carts for the long journey ahead.

"Have you recorded everything?" the keeper of the rest house, a man with gray hair, asked Devendra. The merchant replied with a simple nod.

"And delivery in three days?" the keeper asked.

"Three days if weather permits," Devendra answered. "Four if the rains have softened the road."

The keeper grunted approval and made a small mark on his wooden board. The guild had always kept close track of journeys. Merchants traveled under its name as much as their own. If one of them failed or cheated, it reflected on all.

In less than an hour, Devendra finished preparing his cart. It was pulled by two oxen, their horns wrapped in strips of cloth to avoid chafing. He then climbed up to the driver's plank and flicked the reins lightly. The cart creaked forward, bringing Devendra onto the road outside Ujjain.

The route was alive in a quiet way. Not far into his journey, Devendra passed a group of farmers. Driving a herd of cattle with sticks, they were heading toward the city. Then, Devendra came upon a small group of monks. They wore nothing but simple robes. Their feet were bare, and each of them carried an alms bowl. The monks did not stop Devendra; they rarely asked merchants for anything directly. But often, merchants with a heart would slow their carts and offer a little something to these monks. Devendra took a small packet of grain from his supplies and passed it to the last monk in line. The monk accepted it with a bow and a small smile, then continued without a word. Devendra always reminded himself that giving a little away on the road never harmed a trader's fortunes. If anything, it kept the journey lighter in ways that did not show up in ledgers.

A few hours later, Devendra's journey brought him to a landscape of fields of millet and barley, accompanied by groves of neem and banyan. The road turned so narrow there that only one cart could pass at a time. Farther up, Devendra came across another convoy approaching from the opposite direction. There were three carts in total, each ladened with pottery and baskets of grain.

Their leader raised a hand in greeting. "How is the road east?" he asked when they drew close.

"Dry enough," Devendra replied. "But I heard from the keeper that a small bridge near the second ford has weakened. Cross with care."

"I see. Well, in the west, bandits have been seen near the old mango grove," the other merchant warned. "It is wise to travel with a company."

They exchanged no more than that. Information on the road was as valuable as any coin and traded just as carefully. The carts passed, each man carrying the other's warnings with him.

The temperature shot up by late morning, draining Devendra's energy. Knowing that exhaustion would soon come if he continued the journey, the merchant pulled the cart off the main road and headed toward a roadside shelter built by a local landholder. The resting spot was humble—nothing more than a raised platform with a thatched roof and a stone trough nearby. But it was enough to catch a break.

Devendra unyoked the oxen and led them to drink from the trough. He then sat on the platform to eat. His midday meal was simple: two pieces of wheat flatbread, a handful of lentils cooked the night before, and water carried in a leather bottle. As he chewed, he watched the road and weighed the remaining distance. If the oxen held steady, he would reach the next toll station by late afternoon.

When the worst of the midday heat had passed, he loaded the cart again and returned to the road. As he expected, by late afternoon, a small structure came into view. This was a toll point where local officials collected fees for the use of the road and the nearby river crossing.

"Where are you headed?" one of the officials asked, eyeing the cart.

"Toward the eastern market town," Devendra said, handing over a small tablet that listed his goods.

The man glanced at it, then at the bundles on the cart. "Cotton, pepper, copperware. Guild-registered?"

"Ujjain cloth merchants' śreṇī," Devendra confirmed.

The official nodded, then named the toll. Devendra counted out the coins from a cloth pouch, watching carefully as the man checked each piece. Toll keepers had been known to complain of short payment if a merchant did not pay attention. But today, the exchange was smooth. The barrier was lifted, and Devendra moved on.

After crossing a shallow river ford, the landscape changed once more. Small market villages appeared at intervals, each marked by a cluster of stalls and a shrine beneath a spreading tree. Textile dyers worked near the water, stirring vats of color that stained their hands deep blue and red. Potters' wheels spun lazily as the workers shaped wet clay into jars. Smiths could be seen hunching over small furnaces, expertly coaxing iron into tools and nails.

Devendra did not stop long in these villages. He had arrangements to keep farther along the route. Still, he noted prices overheard at stalls, glimpsed the quality of cloth on local looms, and stored away the faces of possible future buyers.

Only when sky began to turn purple did Devendra reach a familiar and modest market outpost. Merchants like himself often slept here precisely because it lay at the right distance for a three-day delivery. By the time Devendra arrived, the veranda was already full of guild merchants spreading out their beddings close to their carts and goods.

Devendra ended up spending several minutes searching for a spot for the night. He found a narrow corner beside a shop where iron tools hung from a wooden beam. After tending to his oxen, he opened his ledger by the light of an oil lamp set on a stone niche. He tallied the tolls paid, checked his coin pouch, and reviewed the route left for tomorrow. A fellow merchant leaned over, asking the price he planned to charge for his copper vessels. Devendra answered briefly, keeping his calculations precise. When he finally ate a bowl of warm rice and lentils from a local cook, he did so quickly, mindful of the distance still ahead. As the market outpost settled into quiet murmurs and flickering lamps, Devendra lay down on his mat. The Uttarāpatha stretched forward in the darkness, and he intended to follow it at first light. The delivery deadline was close, but it seemed like weather was indeed on his side. Devendra would certainly complete his delivery on time.

A Widow in a Gupta Household

Kamala was already awake before the rest of the house came alive. However, it was more out of habit than necessity. Years ago, when her husband was still alive, she had risen early to prepare for his day. But after his passing, she lived in her eldest son's home. Although her duties had become lighter, it seemed difficult for her to change her routine; it was as if she could not sit still.

And so, she wrapped her plain cotton *sārī* more tightly around her shoulders and made her way into the courtyard, toward the small household shrine set into a niche in the wall. A tiny stone image of Lakṣmī sat there between two oil lamps. The first thing she did was clean the niche. She removed the wilted flowers, relit the lamps, and placed a few grains of rice before the divine image. Then, she whispered her prayer; Kamala wished nothing more than a steady household where neither quarrels nor misfortunes would ever visit.

Then, she went to the kitchen area, where a faint crackle of kindling soothed her aged ears. Her daughter-in-law, Vatsalā, had just started the morning fire. Kamala walked over, not to take over but to watch and assist where needed. A few steps away from them was a younger maid who was busy grinding grain on the stone mill. Kamala warmly greeted her and checked the texture of the grain with her fingertips.

"Add a little more water, and it should bind better," Kamala said gently.

The young maid nodded and adjusted the mixture without complaint. She had always valued Kamala's advice and adored the old woman, for she never raised her voice.

The family began to wake one by one. Her son, Devadatta, stepped into the courtyard, adjusting his upper cloth and rubbing his eyes. He greeted his mother with a respectful morning wish, then moved toward the well for his own washing. A moment later, grandchildren burst from their room, eager to start the day. But Kamala was quick enough to intercept them, smoothing their hair and straightening their garments before they ran too far.

"You need to wash your face first," she said. "Only then may you argue over who sits where."

They smiled sheepishly and obeyed. Small directives like these were hers to give. Indeed, they were not commands of great consequence, but they kept the day's rhythm intact.

Next came breakfast. It was simple. Each filled their stomach with rice porridge, a bit of lentil stew, and buttermilk—typical food enjoyed by those in the Gupta Empire. Everyone ate seated on the floor along the veranda that overlooked the courtyard. Kamala helped her daughter-in-law distribute the bowls, then took her place at the end of the line. She ate last, as custom dictated for widows and elders in many households.

After the bowls were cleared and the younger children shooed away to play, Kamala fetched a small wooden writing board from a shelf. Her grandson, only six, had begun learning his letters. The formal teacher would come later in the week, but she did not mind providing him with daily practice.

"Come and sit, dear one," she said, patting the mat beside her.

He sat cross-legged, eyes following her hand as she traced the first syllable with a reed pen dipped in blackened water. She guided his fingers to follow the strokes. The letters came out crooked and uneven, but Kamala did not scold her grandson.

"Again," she simply said.

As he tried once more, she glanced across the courtyard. Vatsalā was supervising the maid, who was hanging wet clothes along a rope. The younger woman's bracelets jingled faintly. In contrast, Kamala wore nothing around her wrist except for two thin copper bangles. She owned more elaborate jewelry, but she never wore them after her husband's death. Her brightly dyed garments had been put away, too. These days, she only wore *sārīs* that drew no attention: plain, mostly white or pale in color.

Such restraint in dress was common among widows in many respectable urban households of the time. This tradition was shaped by long-standing Brahmanical ideas that linked color and ornament to marital status. But of course, not every widow in Gupta India lived with this degree of austerity. Customs varied depending on the different regions and communities on the subcontinent.

Near midmorning, a neighbor appeared at the doorway, lifting the curtain politely before entering.

"Kamala, have you heard?" she asked after offering a brief greeting. "They say there will be special recitations at the Viṣṇu temple this evening. The priest from the next village is visiting."

Kamala listened, nodding. She asked a few quiet questions, including the exact timing, the offerings needed, and which families had already pledged oil for the lamps. Details mattered in these things. Once the neighbor left, Kamala called her daughter-in-law.

"If you plan to go," she said, "set aside some sesame oil. And ask Devadatta to confirm the hour when he returns from the office. The children should not be taken too late."

Vatsalā nodded, grateful for the clarity. Decisions about temple visits and offerings were technically her husband's to proclaim, but it was Kamala who smoothed them into everyday life.

By late afternoon, Devadatta returned home from his duties. He brought news of a minor tax adjustment and a rumor about an incoming skirmish in a distant province. Kamala listened to her son, but without pressing for details. After all, politics no longer directly concerned her. Still, she knew that news like this was not to be taken lightly. She knew how an empire could change when men spoke in lowered voices and money had to stretch farther than before. The tone in Devadatta's words told her enough.

Suddenly, one of her grandchildren developed a mild cough. Concerned, Kamala quickly sent for the local *vaidya* (physician), who arrived later with a small cloth bag filled with jars and packets. Kamala greeted him respectfully, then stood slightly to one side as he examined the child, listening to his chest and peering at his tongue.

"Thankfully, there is nothing serious," the vaidya said. "The young one spent too much time shouting in the courtyard and not enough resting." He prescribed a simple decoction of herbs and warm water.

Kamala caught his eye. "How often do I feed him this?"

"Twice a day," he replied. "Morning and night, just until the cough settles."

She nodded, committing the instructions to memory. Later, as Vatsalā prepared the remedy, Kamala hovered nearby, checking the quantities and making sure the vessel was clean. She did not take over, but she refused to stand idle.

In the evening, the family began discussing the matter of the recitation about to take place at the Viṣṇu temple. The children were excited to participate, so Devadatta agreed to take them and his wife. Adhering to his mother's request, Devadatta promised to return before it grew too late. Kamala herself chose to stay behind, as she preferred the quieter hours at home now.

After they left, the house felt unusually still. After finishing her chores, the young maid retired to her room. Kamala, on the other hand, still had energy. She walked slowly through the rooms, making sure everything was where it should be, from the grain jars that lined the shelves to the stools in the kitchen and the pots that hung there. She made adjustments where necessary; these small adjustments calmed her more than any long conversation could.

In the courtyard, the light had faded to a deep blue. Kamala picked up a small *dīpa* (oil lamp used for lighting and simple rituals), filled it with a little sesame oil, and adjusted the cotton wick. She lit it from the flame at the household shrine and placed it in the center of the courtyard, then lit two more for the inner rooms. The glow was soft but enough to hold back the darkness.

Then, she lowered herself onto the veranda, knees creaking slightly, and sat with her back against a pillar. For a few moments, she did nothing but simply listened to her surroundings. She could hear the distant murmur of neighbors, the occasional call of a street vendor, and the faint sound of temple bells carried on the evening air. No one called for her, and no decision urgently required her voice, yet she felt content.

When her family finally returned, Kamala immediately stood to receive them. She asked brief, pointed questions about the temple ritual, to which her grandchildren responded with lengthy descriptions. Then, once everyone had eaten and drifted off to their respective rooms, she returned to the courtyard one last time.

She checked that the main *dīpa* still had a little oil, nudged the wick to prolong its life, and adjusted the edge of her *sārī* against the slight night breeze. These actions were nothing remarkable—just one of those small things she did without thinking, keeping the home calm and cared for in ways most people never spoke of but depended on all the same.

Conclusion

You have finally reached the last section of this book, and by now, you should have noticed something: The story of ancient India has way more mysteries than you might ever expect. The deeper you go, the more the ground moves. Answers lead to new questions, and familiar names suddenly gain new details. For a land so old, India surely is full of surprises.

Take the story of the Harappan civilization, for instance. No one was aware of its existence for centuries. Ancient cities lay hidden under soil and riverbeds until archaeologists in the nineteenth century realized that the mounds they had been surveying were more than just ordinary ruins. Planned streets, bead workshops, advanced drainage systems, seals, pottery, a mysterious script—an entire urban area came back into view after thousands of years of silence.

The discoveries have not slowed down. In fact, ancient sites like Rakhigarhi, Dholavira, Bhirrana, and Lothal continue to add something new. Sometimes these discoveries confirm what scholars suspected, and sometimes they overturn almost everything they have confidently confirmed.

The same can also be said of the Mauryan period. Chandragupta, Chanakya, and Ashoka are names that seem familiar. However, the details surrounding these figures keep changing as new interpretations and findings emerge. Ashoka's edicts, scattered across rocks and pillars, continue to be re-read as scholars compare languages, regions, and clues. Archaeologists still debate the exact layout of ancient Mauryan cities and religious centers. Even records of the supposedly well-documented Mauryan state still hold gaps that modern research is trying to fill.

While the Gupta era is celebrated for its beautiful art, literature, and impressive scientific advances, the period also had its own set of uncertainties. Coins, inscriptions, temple remnants, and texts still spark debates among historians and scholars alike. How wealthy were they, really? How stable? How interconnected was the empire with the rest of Asia or the lands beyond the Mediterranean? Each year, new studies adjust our understanding.

Even India's oldest stories behave the same way. Famous epics like the *Mahābhārata* and the *Rāmāyaṇa* are filled with exaggeration, grand battles, impossible weapons, and of course, supernatural beings. Yet, when scholars and archaeologists examine them carefully, some details begin to line up with reality. Ancient place names, descriptions of rivers, references to tribes, hints of migrations—these fragments sometimes match what research uncovers. These epics may not be literal histories, but they also remember.

And that is the real charm of studying ancient India. It refuses to sit still. There are still ruins waiting and inscriptions to be deciphered. And, who knows, maybe the next detail that reshapes what we know about ancient India will come from a place no one thought to look. History, after all, has a habit of surprising us when we least expect it.

Here's another book by Matt Clayton that you might like

Free Bonus from Captivating History (Available for a Limited time)

Hi History Lovers!

Now you have a chance to join our exclusive history list so you can get your first history ebook for free as well as discounts and a potential to get more history books for free!

Simply visit the link below to join.

Or, Scan the QR code!

captivatinghistory.com/ebook

Also, make sure to follow us on Facebook, X, and YouTube by searching for Captivating History.

Bibliography

Anand, Prakriti. "The King Whose Dream Was to Create Hell on Earth: The Story of Ashoka's Hell from Ancient India." *Medium*, May 23, 2025. https://medium.com/@prakritipassion/the-king-whose-dream-was-to-create-hell-on-earth-the-story-of-ashokas-hell-from-ancient-india-659c15282391.

"Ancient Civilizations: India." *National Geographic.* Accessed November 16, 2025.

https://education.nationalgeographic.org/resource/ancient-civilizations-india/.

"Ashoka the Great - Rise of the Mauryan Empire Documentary." Posted April 18, 2019, by

Kings and Generals. *YouTube*, 17 min., 51 sec. www.youtube.com/watch?v=Ed6UZtVTI64.

Bin Naveed, Muhammad. "White Huns (Hephthalites)." *World History Encyclopedia*, June

22, 2015. www.worldhistory.org/White_Huns_(Hephthalites).

"Chanakya: The Political Genius Who Orchestrated the Rise of the Mauryas." Posted May 9,

2022, by Odd Compass. *YouTube*, 16 min., 34 sec. www.youtube.com/watch?v=gAeXw-txPLs.

Datta, Saurav Ranjan. "Ajatashatru." *World History Encyclopedia*, December 18, 2019.

www.worldhistory.org/Ajatashatru.

"Gupta Empire - Golden Age of Classical India - Ancient Civilizations." Posted October 22,

2024, by Kings and Generals. *YouTube*, 18 min., 58 sec. www.youtube.com/watch?v=Vu7myRpw4m4.

"The Hephthalites - Who Were These People and What Do We Known About Them so Far."

Posted February 28, 2024, by Boring Old History. *YouTube*, 22 min., 10 sec. www.youtube.com/watch?v=U2qHaAPQvvo.

Holmes, Robert. "Alexander the Great in India: Furthest and Final Conquests 327-325 BCE."

The Collector, December 4, 2021.

www.thecollector.com/alexander-the-great-india-conquest-achaemenid-empire.

"Indus Valley 3D: Walk the Streets of a 5000-year-old Civilization." Posted July 26, 2025,

by Odd Compass. *YouTube*, 33 min., 18 sec. www.youtube.com/watch?v=bBbE4iOm4cs.

"Introduction to the Story about the Elder Nun Kuṇḍalakesā." Ancient Buddhist Texts.

Accessed November 25, 2025.

https://ancient-buddhist-texts.net/English-Texts/Foremost-Elder-Nuns/09-Kundalakesa.htm.

Manhar, Sharma. "Dasarajna War (Battle of Ten Kings)." *Manhar Sharma* (blog), February

7, 2020. www.manharsharma.com/post/dasarajna-war-battle-of-ten-kings.

Mingren, Wu. "The Rise of Chandragupta Maurya, and the Golden Age of the Mauryan Empire." *Ancient Origins*, May 31, 2023.

www.ancient-origins.net/history-famous-people/chandragupta-maurya-002277.

"Porus: The Indian King Who Confronted Alexander the Great." *World History Edu*,

December 31, 2024. https://worldhistoryedu.com/porus-the-indian-king-who-confronted-alexander-the-great/.

"The Origins of War in Ancient India 5,000 BC—300 BC." Posted December 10, 2023, by

SandRhoman History. *YouTube*, 22 min., 12 sec. www.youtube.com/watch?v=KukBH8eyVOU.

Szczepanski, Kallie. "Biography of Chandragupta Maurya, Founder of the Mauryan Empire."

ThoughtCo, July 3, 2019. www.thoughtco.com/chandragupta-maurya-195490.

Vredeveld, Peter. "Ashoka - Preacher of Buddhism." *Original Buddhas.* Accessed November

20, 2025. www.originalbuddhas.com/blog/ashoka-the-great-emperor.

Wasson, Donald. L. "Battle of Hydaspes." *World History Encyclopedia,* February 26, 2014.

www.worldhistory.org/article/660/battle-of-hydaspes.

Image Sources

1 Hafiz Mujahid Raza, CC BY-SA 4.0 <https://creativecommons.org/licenses/by-sa/4.0>, via Wikimedia Commons: https://commons.wikimedia.org/wiki/File:Ravi_River,_Lahore.jpg

2 https://commons.wikimedia.org/wiki/File:Defeat_of_Porus_by_the_Macedonians.jpg

3 https://commons.wikimedia.org/wiki/File:Le_Brun,_Alexander_and_Porus.jpg

4 Metropolitan Museum of Art, CC0, via Wikimedia Commons: https://commons.wikimedia.org/wiki/File:MET_1984_482_237872.jpg

5 Muhammad Bin Naveed, CC BY-SA 3.0 <https://creativecommons.org/licenses/by-sa/3.0>, via Wikimedia Commons: https://commons.wikimedia.org/wiki/File:Another_view_of_Granary_and_Great_Hall_on_Mound_F.JPG

6 Avantiputra7, CC BY-SA 3.0 <https://creativecommons.org/licenses/by-sa/3.0>, via Wikimedia Commons: https://commons.wikimedia.org/wiki/File:Indus_Valley_Civilization,_Mature_Phase_(2600-1900_BCE).png

7 Gary Todd, CC0, via Wikimedia Commons: https://commons.wikimedia.org/wiki/File:Harappan_(Indus_Valley)_Balance_%26_Weights.jpg

8 Gaffar772, CC BY-SA 4.0 <https://creativecommons.org/licenses/by-sa/4.0>, via Wikimedia Commons: https://commons.wikimedia.org/wiki/File:Moen_Jo_Daro_(The_Mond_of_the_Deads).jpg

9 Avantiputra7, CC BY-SA 3.0 <https://creativecommons.org/licenses/by-sa/3.0>, via Wikimedia Commons: https://commons.wikimedia.org/wiki/File:Nanda_Empire,_c.325_BCE.png

10 https://commons.wikimedia.org/wiki/File:Chanakya_artistic_depiction.jpg

11 https://commons.wikimedia.org/wiki/File:Ruins_of_Patliputra_at_Kumhrar.JPG

12 Photo Dharma from Sadao, Thailand, CC BY 2.0
   <https://creativecommons.org/licenses/by/2.0>, via Wikimedia Commons:
   https://commons.wikimedia.org/wiki/File:Ashoka%27s_visit_to_the_Ramagrama_st
   upa_Sanchi_Stupa_1_Southern_gateway.jpg

13 https://commons.wikimedia.org/wiki/File:Dhauli_Ashoka_inscription_
   Puri_District_India.jpg

14 User:BPG, CC BY-SA 2.5 <https://creativecommons.org/licenses/by-sa/2.5>, via
   Wikimedia Commons: https://commons.wikimedia.org/wiki/File:Bimbisarajail.jpg

15 https://commons.wikimedia.org/wiki/File:Draupadi_and_Pandavas.jpg

16 Gita Press Gorakhpur, CC0, via Wikimedia Commons:
   https://commons.wikimedia.org/wiki/File:Sit_with_Rama.jpg

17 https://commons.wikimedia.org/wiki/File:Asoka%27s_Queen.jpg

18 Nomu420, CC BY-SA 3.0 <https://creativecommons.org/licenses/by-sa/3.0>, via
   Wikimedia Commons: https://commons.wikimedia.org/wiki/File:Amrapali_
   greets_Buddha_Roundel_36_buddha_ivory_tusk.jpg

19 Bernard Gagnon, CC BY-SA 3.0 <https://creativecommons.org/licenses/by-sa/3.0>,
   via Wikimedia Commons:
   https://commons.wikimedia.org/wiki/File:Shri_Ram_Ghat_01.jpg

www.ingramcontent.com/pod-product-compliance
Lightning Source LLC
Chambersburg PA
CBHW060635080726
47818CB00004B/158